COCKNEY RABBIT

Dedicated to the loving memory of
Violet Puxley
1915–93

Heaven is a nicer place for her being there

MORE COCKNEY RABBIT

A DICK 'N' ARRY OF CONTEMPORARY RHYMING SLANG

Ray Puxley

ROBSON BOOKS

First published in Great Britain in 1998 by Robson Books,
The Chrysalis Building, Bramley Road, London, W10 6SP

An imprint of Chrysalis Books Group plc

British Library Cataloguing in Publication Data
A catalogue record for this title is available from the British Library.

ISBN 1 86105 730 X

Printed by Creative Print & Design (Wales), Ebbw Vale

Introduction

In the years since *Cockney Rabbit* was published in 1992, there has been a tremendous upsurge in the use of rhyming slang. Its popularity has arisen not out of necessity for a secret language but as a way of brightening up the English language. Many would argue that our tongue is bright enough and, in the hands of our great pencil wallahs, past and present, I would not disagree. But the everyday speech of the common man is, in the main, unexceptional but functional. The use of a colourful word substitute livens things up a bit and seldom fails to amuse, but it is no longer the sole property of the Cockney.

Modern terms are springing up daily and the source is often miles away from the East End, in suburbia. It has even been suggested that rhyming slang has been hijacked by the middle classes. Well, I don't know about that but they have certainly embraced it and added to it with terms like Germaine Greer, Charles Dance, Calvin Klein, Schindler's List and Eros & Cupid.

By far the main breeding ground is among the young working classes where the bulk of the terms again take on the names of the famous, indicating a celebrity-dominated culture. Comedian Jack Dee shares a toilet with film star Brad Pitt, while politician John Gummer shares a term with rock star Joe Strummer. Sportsmen, Gianluca Vialli and Niki Laudar get up people's noses, often in the joint domain of tennis menace Ilie Nastase and weird Mother, Frank Zappa.

The test, of course, is time. Some will remain on the tongue, others will vanish as many already have. The fact that more are being recorded these days will help but who knows how many undocumented examples have come and gone?

It would come as no surprise to learn that, in the sixties, people drove their Ringo Starrs or rode their Dick Van Dykes to the I'm a Loser for a Lily the Pink and maybe some Hey Jude, making sure that they washed their Mary Rands before eating their Yul Brynner. They may later have paid a visit to the Riki Tiki Tavi for a Simon Dee or an Ingrid Pitt, or just to powder their Monica Rose before getting on their Cassius Clay, probably risking a tug by the War & Peace and having to blow in a Bottle of Tizer.

I have done my best to keep abreast with the modern terms but with so many personalities with rhymeable names and so many people ready to make a connection, it is an impossibility to keep up with it all.

I would like to thank all the people who wrote to me with their examples following *Cockney Rabbit*, especially for the contribution made by Geoffrey Gwilliam. My best plates and dishes to you all.

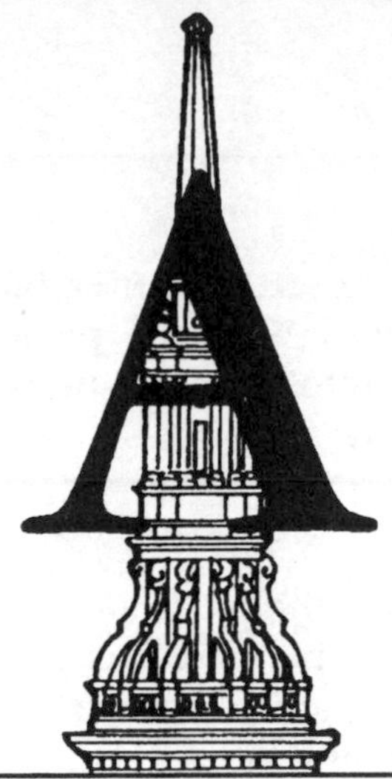

Aberdeen(s) ***Bean(s)***

Mainly applies to baked beans but also serves as a Spoonerism on 'ad a bean, whereby the hungry may moan: 'I'm starving, I haven't Aberdeen all day.'

Abraham ***Sham***

Pronounced Abram, this applies to getting out of something by feigning illness. Many have 'gone on the Abram' by phoning in sick, only to be seen at a televised race meeting, grinning like a gom behind John McCrirrick.

Adam & Eve ***1 Believe***

Very old and very common and often an expression of disbelief, e.g., 'I can't Adam and Eve you said that.'

2 Leave

When it's time to go, it's time you were 'Adam & Eveing'.

After Eight Mint ***Skint***
What the after-dinner bachelor is by Monday morning. With the promotion of Boracic Lint almost into mainstream English, 'after eight' has joined the firm.

Ajax ***Tax***
Based on the name of the ancient Greek warrior who later became a scouring powder and a Dutch football team. Now, in the shape of a disc, he is to be seen on a car windscreen. Or should be!

Alabaster ***Plaster***
Always said as 'ala', this is the lowest rung of the most convoluted ladder in RS. When you reach the top you'll find yourself at the bottom. *See* PLASTER OF PARIS.

Alan Ladd ***Sad***
As well as in a sense of dejection, i.e., 'What's up? You look a bit Alan Ladd,' this may also be heard in relation to someone referred to these days as an 'anorak'. Anyone who, by choice, knows the difference in widths of any two given railway tracks in the world is laughed off as being 'a bit Alan Ladd really'. Based on an American film star (1913–64).

Alan Whicker ***Nicker (£1)***
An 'Alan' is a piece of newspeak lowspeak.

Alderman's Nail ***Tail***
A very old term concerning a dog's wagpiece, as in, 'as happy as a dog with two aldermans'.

Alf Garnett ***Barnet***

An example of how, when a piece becomes as common as Barnet Fair (hair), it acquires a term of its own, just to make things more interesting. Good to see one of the all-time famous Cockneys involved in RS, even if, with Alf having a headful of bald, it is a bit unsuitable.

Alfred the Great ***Weight***

Always reduced to 'Alfred' by those wishing to reduce their 'Alfred'. Based on the old king of Wessex (849–99) who was famous for burning cakes, not calories.

Ali Oop ***Poop (Excrement)***

Coined from the phrase shouted at the performance of a feat, most commonly on stage. To the accompaniment of a splash, it may also be heard in the toilet after a long, eye-bulging struggle to bring a bout of constipation to an end.

For an explanation as to why being constipated is known as 'having a bung in the bottle' and why a laxative is a 'bottle opener', you need to know that in RS, 'bottle and glass' means 'arse'.

All Quiet on the Western Front ***Cunt***

An old but long-silent term of abuse, probably from the army, where 'All quiet' may have meant 'officer coming'.

Anthea Turner ***Earner***

On television this famous-for-being-famous personality may appear all sweetness and light, but in RS she's money made, usually from a no-questions-asked deal.

Apricot & Peach ***Beach***

A Cockney lad on a 'yoof' holiday in Spain was heard to suggest that, 'We go down the apricot, get some currant and look at the lemons.' Whether he had a fruitful afternoon or not is not recorded. (Currant Bun - Sun; Lemon Curds - Birds.)

April in Paris ***Aris***

A piece that is three times removed from its meaning, namely the shit chute. (Aristotle - Bottle; Bottle and Glass - Arse.)

Artichoke ***Smoke***

In its original form this was an 'Artichoke Ripe', a pipe, and dates back to a time when pipe smoking was more widespread than it is today. By ridding the term of its second element it now applies to any form of smoking. One of the cleverer pieces of RS, it suggests that the originator was coughing his giblets up when he coined it, i.e., having a hearty choke.

Artichoke Ripe ***Pipe***
An ancient piece that has run out of puff.

Ascot Races ***Braces***
Known as 'Ascots' but probably not to the titfer brigade who gather here during 'the season'.

Aston Villa ***Pillow/Pillar***
Since both words are pronounced the same, an 'Aston' is equally at home as either the thing you rest your weary filbert on or the view obstructer at a football match.

Auntie Ella ***Umbrella***
An infrequent term for a mush.

Aunt Maria ***Fire***
An old piece that went out when Old King Coal ceased to rule the fireplace.

Baby's Pap ***Cap***

First recorded in mid nineteenth century, when the working man was particularly adept at turning out children and wearing flat hats, often at the same time. Hence the connection.

Bacon Rind ***Blind***

A not-too-common piece that is used in the same way as 'mutton' is for deaf. (Mutt and Jeff – Deaf.)

Backseat Driver ***Skiver***

A fitting piece for one who doesn't want to do the work but will tell you how it should be done.

Back-Wheel Skid ***Yid***

A 'back wheeler' is a sometimes-used alternative to a 'front wheeler'. Same meat, different gravy.

Bag of Coke ***Poke (Sexual Intercourse)***

Possibly from the old illusion that the coalman was

often paid in kind, as in the saying, 'never be unfaithful with the milkman when you're in debt to the coalman.'

Bag of Fruit ***Suit***
An old example that only fits properly when it isn't shortened. You're always cased up in your best 'bag o' fruit'.

Bag of Sand ***Grand (£1000)***
A 'bag' is of recent coinage in the City of London.

Balaclava ***Charver (Sexual Intercourse)***
A sinister term. Charver comes from a Romany word for the taking of a woman, and a balaclava has become a symbol of the rapist. The connection is probably unintentional, a fortuitous rhyme used chauvinistically or, as they say today, laddishly.

Banana Fritter ***Shitter (Lavatory)***
The place to accommodate one suffering a bout of the BANANA SPLITS (qv).

Banana Split(s) ***Shit(s)***
Always used in the first element whereby you may go for a 'banana' or have a touch of them.

Bangers & Mash ***Slash***
A 'bangers' is one of the many terms for urination on stream.

Barney Rubble ***Trouble***
Not to be confused with the long-standing 'barney' meaning a fight. Fred Flintstone's oppo lends his name to a spot of bother, whereby antagonizing the wife will land you in a bit of 'Barney' with the 'trouble'. *See* TROUBLE AND STRIFE.

Beecham's Pill ***Still***
A professional snapper's term for a photograph.

Beef Heart ***Fart***
An offering from the offal counter for back-end backfire.

Bell Ringer(s) ***Finger(s)***
Try ringing a bell without them!

Benny Hill ***1 Drill***
A carpenter, when asked if there was a reason why his power drill had become identified with the great British comedian (1926–92) replied, 'They both bore a bit.' Obviously not a fan.

2 Till
A modern term for a cash register based on the man whose comic persona would have enjoyed having his buttons pushed by young women at the checkout.

Big Mac ***Sack***
A contemporary term for dismissal from work, from a type of hamburger.

Billy Goat ***Coat***
A rarely heard alternative to the female of the species. *See* NANNY GOAT.

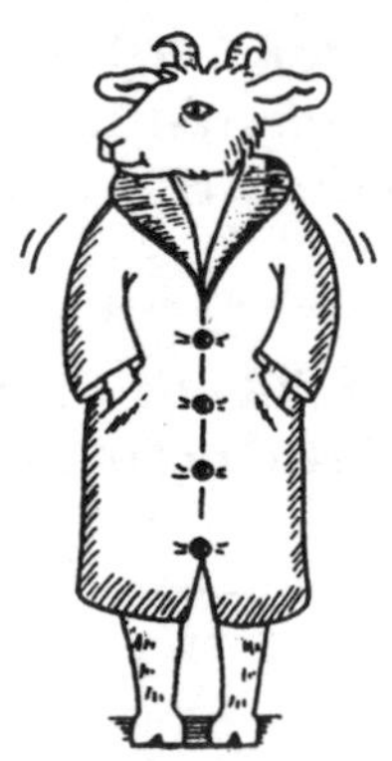

Billy Liar(s) ***Tyre(s)***
From the sixties film of the same name, this is quite apt in that a flat 'Billy' is often a moody excuse for being late.

Black & Decker ***Pecker (Penis)***
Taken from the name of a company that produces power tools, this would appear to refer to the equipment of a sexual marathon man. 'Course, the name is also synonymous with DIY. This is pecker in its American form and should not be confused with the older British version meaning the nose, an extension of beak. 'Keep your pecker up' conveys a totally different message in the States.

Blackwall Tunnel ***Funnel***
An old term from the docks for a ship's chimney. The Blackwall Tunnel, known locally as the 'pipe' or 'conduit', runs under the Thames between Poplar and Greenwich. At peak times it is a motorist's nightmare and so has accumulated many other names as well. Usually two words, the first one beginning with F.

Bladder of Fat ***Hat***
An out-of-date example that probably referred to greasy headwear that sat upon greasy heads.

Block & Tackle ***Shackle (Handcuffs)***
Originally referred to fetters but got hoisted up from ankles to wrists a long time ago.

Blueberry Hill ***Bill (Police)***
Based on a famous hit record in the fifties, the 'blueberry' is a recent piece heard on a TV drama.

Board and Plank *Yank*
Must have some connection with the actors on those dire daytime American soaps hidden away on satellite television.

Bobby Moore *Door*
Modern piece coined by football fans, too young to have seen West Ham and England's great World Cup winning captain (1941-93)

Botany Bay *Hay*
A very old piece that cabmen may have fed to their horses, but it mainly refers to sleeping, whereby to 'hit the Botany' was the intention of the weary.

Bottle of Booze *Twos (Odds of 2/1)*
There seems to be some contention as to whether this or Bottle of Spruce is responsible for the common expression 'bottle' in this sense, which goes back to the early days of greyhound racing. In its heyday, the 'dogs' attracted huge crowds of working-class men, every one of them an expert on *canis swifticus*. An old ditty, 'A Dog's Widow's Lament' went :

Now the dogs have started
The boys won't go to work
They want to be a tic-tac
They want to be a clerk
Bunkie-doodle-ido
Take five to four.

Bottle of Kola *Bowler*
An old term for the city gent's attire that is now old hat.

Bottle of Scent *Bent (Homosexual)*
Comes from a time when men were considered

poofy if they smelt of anything other than soap and sweat,

Bottle of Water ***1 Daughter***
When daddy hears he's got a little girl for a daughter this is just the stuff to wet the baby's head with, I don't think!

2 Quarter
In the dingy world of drugs this is a quarter of an ounce.

Bottle of Wine ***Fine***
A term, laid down some years ago, which refers to a punishment as poured by a magistrate.

Bow & Arrow ***1 Sparrow***
A bird much in the affection of Londoners.

2 Charra
When the early form of motor coach was known as a charabanc, it was soon reduced to a charra, only to make the transition to a Bow and Arrer.

Brad Pitt ***Shit***
A totally new piece which will probably not go down too well with this American film star. But that won't stop people going for a Brad Pitt.

Bread and Butter ***1 Gutter***
Very old example when used in relation to being down and out or 'in the bread and butter'.

2 Nutter
A newer adaptation when referring to anyone that is a stump short of a wicket.

3 Putter
A television golf commentator's term.

4 Stutter
A term not easily said by one with this speech impediment.

Brenda Frickers ***Knickers***
A modern piece for what's found in the drawers drawer known as 'Brendas', after an Irish TV and film actress.

Brighton Line ***Nine***
Mince pies down for another number on the bingo card of RS.

Brighton Rock ***Dock***
The 'Brighton' is that part of a courtroom where the accused learns if he is to spend some time at one of HM's guest houses.

Broken Heart ***Fart***
Probably from the rhyme scrawled on many a lavatory wall:

Here I sit broken hearted
Spent a penny and only farted.

Bromley by Bow ***Dough (Money)***
A cab driver's term based on an area of East London. Always short changed to 'Bromley'.

Bronze Figure ***Kipper***
An imperfect rhyme that finds itself carved up by Jack the Ripper.

Brother & Sister ***Blister***
As seen on the hands after a rare burst of hard graft or on the feet as a result of tight shoes or an unaccustomed burst of running.

Bubble Gum ***Bum***
A lovely 'bubble', that of a curvaceous woman.

Buccaneer ***Queer (Homosexual)***
The dictionary defines this early sailor as : 'a pirate, an unscrupulous adventurer'. Well, boys will be boys.

Bully Beef ***1 Chief***
Old reference to a prison warder.

2 Deaf
A term from north of the border that is unlikely to be heard or understood south of it.

Bulrush ***Brush***
A paintbrush, a piece from the painting and decorating trade. These days it pays to be choosy about who you get to do your toshing, the world is awash with ne'er-do-well decorators. In our multi-racial society even Indians can be cowboys. A tosher nowadays is a painter, but in Victorian London he was a slum dweller who made a kind of living searching the sewers for any valuables - usually small coins - which may have fallen through a drain. Anything a tosher found was known as 'tosh', a word that survives today as slang for 'rubbish'. A pocketful of small change, a far-fetched film, or the verbal outpourings of a blowhard, all may be classed as 'a load of tosh'.

Bunsen Burner ***1 Earner***
A nice little tickle that brings in some bunce, that's a 'Bunsen'

2 Turner
A cricketer's term for a pitch that is beneficial to a spin bowler.

Burdett Coutts ***Boots***
An out-of-fashion term based on the philanthropic Angela Burdett-Coutts, whose acts of charity must have included putting footwear on the feet of the poor of Victorian Britain.

Burglar Alarm(s) ***Arm(s)***
One of several examples rhyming on 'alarm' that are sending out warning signals to the long-dominant Chalk Farm.

Burlington Bertie ***Thirty***
Another piece from the bingo caller's book of RS, this one based on the shirtless toff from Bow.

Buttered Bread ***Dead***
Heard in a pub:

First man: I see they buried Alfie Smith yesterday.
Second man: (surprised) Is old Alfie buttered bread then?
First man: (sarcastic) No. He's first prize in a treasure hunt.

Buttered Bun ***One***
A bingo caller's alternative to Kelly's eye.

Buttered Scone ***One***
A bingo caller's alternative to the alternative to Kelly's eye. *See* previous entry.

Cab Rank ***Rank***
Apt in a money-goes-to-money sense, although most taxi drivers would deny it.

Cabman's Rest(s) ***Breast(s)***
An old, obsolete piece which shows that cabbies of the past weren't just interested in tips.

Calcutta ***Butter***
A term that seems to be spreading for no other reason than that it rhymes.

Calvin Klein ***1 Fine***
Modern piece of 'yoof' speak for the punishment you might receive if you were caught selling snide designer gear from a fly pitch.

2 Wine
Red or white. Plonk or vintage. It's all 'Calvin' and is based on the American fashion designer.

Camden Lock ***Shock***
A modern example and used as in 'You haven't been to Camden Town for twenty years? You're in for a Camden Lock then.'

Camerer Cuss ***Bus***
A piece that dates back to the early days of omnibus travel, based on the name of the long-established specialists in antique timepieces and jewellery.

Camilla Parker Bowles ***Rolls (Royce)***
Based on the lady friend of the Prince of Wales in relation to the Prince of Wheels, which has become a 'Camilla Parker'. *See also* PARKER BOWLES.

Can of Coke ***Joke***
A contemporary piece of young people talk, where the cheapest 'can of cokes' are usually at someone else's expense. A lad waiting an age to be served in a crowded pub was heard to declare 'This is an effing can o' coke this gaff.'

Captain Bligh ***Pie***
After the old salt famous for the mutiny aboard his ship the *Bounty* in 1789. Against the odds he survived to make mincemeat of the mutineers. William Bligh (1754-1817) later became an admiral before serving as governor of New South Wales.

Captain Cook ***Look***
Not as common as Butcher's Hook but when it is used it is always in full.

Captain Kettle ***Settle***
Based on a comic book hero of a bygone age, this term for putting an end to an argument, by violent

means or otherwise, is no more. These days it's called a straightener.

Captain Kirk ***Turk***
A recent formation due to the popularity of Turkey as a holiday resort.

Captain's Log ***Bog (Lavatory)***
When there are rumblings in the poop deck, an entry in the Captain's Log is warranted.

Cat & Kitty ***Titty***
As displayed, possibly, by the woman who puts her pussy to work in a cat house.

Cat's Milk ***Silk***
Relates to smoothness, hence a malt whisky or a widgetized beer may go down 'as smooth as cat's milk'. I would have thought 'cow's milk' would have been more appropriate. How do you milk a cat? Gingerly I suppose.

Cecil Gee(s) ***Knee(s)***
A fairly old term based on the chain of menswear shops, where the second element always gets discounted, i.e., 'Get down on your Cecils and say a Chocolate Eclair (Prayer).'

Centre Half ***Scarf***
A neck warmer fittingly enough from the football terraces since it's based on the player in the number 5 shirt.

Champagne Glass ***Brass (Prostitute)***
A twice-removed example, for Brass Nail (Tail, prostitute), which is suggestive of the high-class call girl who entertains visiting nobs.

Chandelier ***Queer (Homosexual)***
That which hangs gaily from the ceiling. A chandelier that is. Normally reduced to a 'shandy'.

Channel Fleet ***Street***
A very old piece that seems to have sunk without trace.

Charles Dance ***Chance***
Heard on a long-haul flight:

First man: Want a game of chess?
Second man: No, you always beat me.
First man: All right, I'll give you a Charles Dance.
Second man: How?
First man: I'll play left-handed.

Based on the British actor.

Charles James Fox ***Box***
An ancient piece for a theatrical box that has long been known as a 'Charles James'. Based on Britain's first foreign secretary (1749–1806).

Charlie Clore ***1 Floor***
An old piece from the fight game, where to put an opponent down was to put him on the 'Charlie'.

2 Score (£20)
Based on the name of a millionaire financier to whom this amount would have been tiny taters.

Charlie Cooke ***Look***
A sixties term based on a former Chelsea and Scotland winger who rarely gave full backs a look in.

Charlie Drake(s) ***1 Brake(s)***
It would be interesting to see a fitter's reaction if a woman drove into his garage and asked to have her Charlies looked at.

2 Break
A tea break or rest period courtesy of the comedian who first came to prominence as part of a double act called Mick and Montmorency. Charlie's catchphrase was 'Is it teatime yet?' Therefore an apt example.

Charlie Freer ***Beer***
An old piece that came to the bitter end of its existence long ago.

Charlie Frisky ***Whisky***
Not much left in the bottle for this particular drop of short.

Cheerful Giver ***Liver***
A bosom boozing buddy is one who will see the night out with you, with no consideration for his own 'cheerful giver'.

Cheese & Crackers ***Knackers (Testicles)***
The after-dinner course in relation to a vegetarian's lunchbox, i.e., two veg without the meat.

Cheese Grater ***Waiter***
A fitting piece for the one who sprinkles the Parmesan and acts Kraftily till he gets his tip. I suppose a head waiter is the big cheese is he?

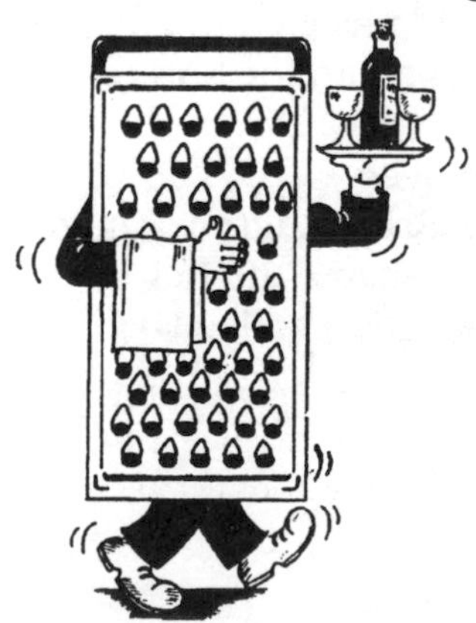

Chelsea Bun ***Son/Son***
From the same oven as several other terms making the same rhyme.

Cheltenham Bold ***Cold***
An old term based on the home of the National Hunt Festival, where old jumpers may fall like the temperature.

Cherry Red ***Head***
'Tampax fugit,' as the drunk said when his wife threw a sanitary towel at his 'cherry'.

Chew the Fat ***Chat***
A well-known piece that has transcended the realms of RS to join the conventional language for a chinwag.

Chicken's Neck ***Cheque***
An alternative to Goose's Neck, probably for a less poultry amount.

Chips and Peas ***Knees***
Some vegetables from the RS menu that sit on the plate of general slang alongside 'Marrers' (Marrow bones), an ancient term for the leg joints.

Chirrup & Titter ***Bitter (Ale)***
An old piece on the lines of 'Giggle and Titter' that has come to the bottom of the barrel.

Christopher Lee ***Pee/Wee***
The British actor, famed for his roles in horror films, shares the bill with a large cast making this connection with a lagg.

Christmas Tree(s) — ***Knee(s)***

The seasonal indoor toilet the dog pines for in cold weather represents those that have been known to tremble behind the bike shed. Not necessarily in cold weather.

Chunk of Beef — ***Chief***

An old reference to somebody in charge that was shortened to a 'chunka'.

Chunk of Wood — ***Good***

A nineteenth-century piece that generally referred to the opposite of good. Anything bad was 'no chunk of wood.'

Cigarette Holder(s) — ***Shoulder(s)***

Heard at a football match on a freezing day:

Her: Got a hanky? My nose keeps running.
Him: No. Use your sleeve.
Her: (annoyed) No. This is my new coat. It cost a lot of money.
Him: Well, I've been using your cigarette.

Cisco Kid — ***Yid***

An old term based on a Western film hero. A cowboy from Mexico as opposed to Stamford Hill.

City Tote — ***Coat***

When summer heads for sunnier climes for the winter, put your 'City Tote' on. A fairly recent piece formed on the name of a bookmaking firm.

Claire Rayners — ***Trainers***

A contemporary term for modern footwear, designed for physical activity, based on an agony aunt who clearly wasn't.

Clodhopper *Copper (Policeman)*
Based on the traditionally perceived size of a lawman's leg-ends - the term being a large heavy shoe - 'Plod the Clod' now pounds the beat. Or, depending on where you live, doesn't.

Come a Clover *Fall/Fell Over*
A First World War term that was probably supremely apt when the bullets were flying, it's what a missing comrade may have done. It was also used as a warning of an impending greenacre, i.e., 'Do your laces up or you'll come a clover.' There's more chance of it snowing in Blackwall Tunnel than coming across it now though.

Cockaleekie *Cheeky*
Based on a type of soup, this is used as a playful warning, e.g., 'Don't get cockaleekie or I'll smack your legs.'

Cod's Roe *Dough (Money)*
A losing punter may often be heard to complain that he has 'done his cod's.'

Comic Singer(s) *Finger(s)*
As rare these days as a comic song.

Con & Col *Dole*
What these two diminutives of 'Colin' have to do with signing on I don't know.

Conger Eel *Squeal*
The slippery fish comes in as an underworld term for what an informer does.

Corned Beef *1 Thief*
A fairly modern piece that hasn't supplanted the evergreen Tea Leaf.

2 Chief
A prison term for the chief warder.

Cotton Wool *Pull*
The hunt for sexual quarry is known as going on the 'cotton'.

Cough and Choke *Smoke*
As a noun or a verb this couldn't be more suitable.

Cousin Sis *Piss*
A very old reference to boozing, i.e., Going on the 'cousin sis'.

Cow & Gate *Late*
When a woman is 'cow & gate' for her period it is usually a sign that she will soon be buying baby food. Hence the name of the pap-producing people. Clever eh?

Cows and Kisses *Missus (Wife)*
In mid-nineteenth century parlance a cow was a common reference to a woman, though not considered as offensive as it is now. So this very old term makes more sense when you understand that it means 'women and kisses'. Unless there was some secret perversion that went undocumented.

Crocodile Dundee *Flea*
Had a slight usage when the film of this name was popular in reference to a dog's boarders, as in 'The dog won't bite you but his crocodiles might.'

Cuddle & Kiss *1 Piss*
Quite common when slashed to be the first element, e.g., 'Watch my beer I'm just going for a cuddle.'

2 Miss
Old, obvious term for a girlfriend. Coined when a kiss and cuddle was all a boy could expect until about the 950th date.

Cuddled and Kissed *Pissed*
The frequently 'cuddled' may wind up addled or puddled.

Currant Bread *Dead*
Should always be used in full, referring to the passed on as 'currant' sounds wrong somehow.

Daily Mail

1 Ale
Going for a pint of 'daily' is a reference to going to the pub.

2 Nail
Mainly employed in the carpentry trade.

3 Tail
This takes in tail in many guises. It's the backside whereby a busy man may 'work his daily off'. It also means to follow when it is common for a PC to be on a suspect's 'daily'. It's the prostitute more commonly associated with Brass Nail and the waggable part of a dog.

4 Tale
As told by a conman or a sneaky snitcher.

5 Bail
An underworld example employing an over-used term.

Damon Hill ***Pill***
The link with Britain's ace motor racer has to relate to speed (amphetamines).

Dan Dares ***Flairs***
The comic-book hero from the future sees action as a pair of strides from the past.

Darky Cox ***Box***
Seating area in the theatre as described by your theatrical type.

Darren Gough ***Cough***
The Yorkshire and England cricketer, who has had his share of injuries, will be as one with ill health for ever more. In the nicest possible way, of course.

Date and Plum ***Bum***
An old term that is always pruned to the first element, e.g.,

Wife: The dog's been full of mischief today.
Husband: Yeah? Well, his date'll be full of my boot if he keeps on.

David Gower ***Shower***
The former England cricket captain lends his name to BO bashing in the bathroom. This is a new term so maybe it will get extended to refer to a sudden cloudburst which would be fitting enough. After all, it wouldn't be the first time he'd come out of the sky to interrupt a cricket match.

Didn't Oughta ***Water***
A very old term, which has not been used for years, could aptly resurface as a warning against swimming in the seas off Britain.

Dirty Face(s) ***Lace(s)***
An old example that puts a spark of humour into such a mundane thing as a shoestring.

(Go) Divine Brown ***(Go) Down (Oral Sex)***
So apt it's like divine providence for the slangman. Ms Brown is the doxy caught by Los Angeles police officers with her face down actor Hugh Grant's trousers.

Dixie Lid ***Kid***
A dixie is an iron cooking pot, used in the army to make military custard, soup, porridge etc. It can also boil eggs en masse for the dipping in of soldiers.

Do As You Like ***Bike***
From a time when cyclists kept to the road and knew what a red light meant. Now they do as they like.

Docker's Hook ***Look***
Oldish but never grabbed the attention away from Butcher's.

Doctor & Nurse ***Purse***
A mugger will snatch a 'doctor' and leg it.

Doctor Legg ***Egg***
Used in a caff by a building worker to the amusement of his pals. When ordering a fry up he asked for two 'Doctor Leggs'. Based on the oft mentioned but seldom seen medic in *EastEnders*.

Dog and Boned ***Stoned***
Known as 'doggo' in connection with someone who is blotto or out of his nut on drugs.

Dolly Mixtures ***Pictures***
Sweets are synonymous with going to the cinema. They usually come in rustly bags which are synonymous with me *leaving* the cinema.

Do Me a Favour ***Neighbour***
An imperfect rhyme but may be a perfectly fitting example if liberty takers live next door. For many the ideal 'do me' is one who's not there when he's not wanted.

Do My Dags ***Fags***
An old and extinguished term based on the name of a children's game which meant 'follow my lead'. Known as 'do mes', and apt in that kids will follow their parents into a cigarette packet.

Don Revie ***Bevvy***
A term coined by boozers of the seventies based on the then manager of the England football team.

Don't Make a Fuss ***Bus***
An ancient term that is as apt today as it ever was, although maybe today it's for different reasons. To make a fuss about the foul-mouthed, loutish behaviour of your fellow passengers is likely to get you a mouthful of abuse or worse. Especially from the schoolchildren.

Doorknob ***1 Bob***
Obsolete in as much as it was used for a shilling.

2 Job
East End Boy Scouts may have incorporated this with ***Bob*** (above) on 'doorknob a doorknob' week.

Door to Door *Four*
Housey to housey.

Doublet & Hose *Nose*
Since actors are the only ones likely to wear this attire, a 'doublet' has to be a theatrical conk-oction. 'You get right up my doublet?' Sounds like it could be.

Douglas Hurd *1 Turd*
A recent term based on the British politician. When a person goes to perform what for a man is a sit down job on the lavatory they have gone to 'dump a Douglas'. Also the one reclining on the pavement waiting to be stepped on.

2 Third
A third class honours degree. A piece of student slang from the eighties.

Dover Boat *Coat*
One to keep you warm on the cross Channel ferry, possibly with deep pockets to hide the duty frees.

Down the Drain(s) *Brain(s)*
May be based on the wasted education of a plank-head, about whom it may be said 'There's none so thick as those who don't want to learn.'

Dripping Toast *Host*
Whereby a publican becomes mine 'dripping'.

Drum and Fife *Wife*
An old term for the old woman that was popular during the First World War. One can only wonder at how many letters were written to a 'drum and fife', but delivered to a widow.

Dublin Trick ***Brick***
Well known on building sites of yore but which has probably been laid to rest.

Duke of York ***1 Cork***
That which seals a bottle.

2 Fork
Refers to the implement but is most readily connected to the hands which have long been known as forks. Hence 'Put up your dukes' has become a familiar expression as a fistic challenge.

3 Talk
Less common than Rabbit and Pork but wasn't always so.

4 Chalk
Was scribbling on the blackboard of RS in the late nineteenth century.

5 Pork
Has been scratching around for a century or so and is still cooking.

6 Walk
Another piece that's been strolling off Cockney tongues for years.

Dutch Plate ***Mate***
Old but less frequently used than China Plate.

Early Door — ***Whore***
An old piece for one who is willing to get her Early Doors (drawers) off.

East & South — ***Mouth***
Was in use before the 'tater trap' underwent a change in direction to the oft spouted North & South.

Easter Bunny — ***Money***
The ball-churning dream machine, which has made 'If I win the lottery' a national catchphrase, provides us with the multi-million to one chance of having enough 'Easter Bunny' to never have to waste it on necessities again. A wish called squander, so to speak.

Easter Egg(s) — ***Leg(s)***
The seasonal confection, on sale on Boxing Day, is another to make the egg/leg connection.

East India Docks ***Socks***
An old example that has probably disappeared under the same bulldozer as the docks.

Eau de Cologne ***1 Phone***
Always shortened to 'the odour' or 'odie'.

2 Palone (Woman)
A theatrical piece of RS for an example of parlyaree.

Edmundo Ros ***Boss***
Based on a Latin American bandleader, seldom off the box in the fifties and sixties.

Egon Ronay ***Pony***
Another piece of slang for slang, whereby to 'go for an Egon' is to defecate. Based on the famed gastronome who knows all the best places to fill up with scran, and now, it seems, where to get rid of it.

Egyptian Hall ***Ball (Dance)***
Based on an exhibition hall which stood in Piccadilly from 1812 until it was demolished in 1905.

Elky Clark ***Mark***
Applies to a starting point or meeting place: 'Be on the Elky at nine.' Based on a Scottish boxer, a British and European flyweight champion of the 1920s. Sometimes said as L. K. CLARK (qv).

Ellen Terry ***Jerry***
An archaic piece formed on the name of a Shakespearian actress (1847–1928) who probably deserves better than to be remembered as a po.

Elton John ***Con***
The recently knighted musician goes on record as any kind of stitch up, tuck up or take on, always as an 'Elton'.

Emmerdale Farm(s) ***Arms(s)***
Based on a long-running television soap opera and, like the programme, RS loses the 'farm', e.g., 'All right if you're twisting my Emmerdale I'll have a double.'

Engelbert Humperdinck ***Drink***
A mouthful from the sixties that is always halved to an 'Engelbert'. After the chart topper of the period who only found fame after scrapping the name of Gerry Dorsey in favour of that of a nineteenth-century German composer.

Eros & Cupid ***Stupid***
A piece from the middle classes whereby the Greek and Roman love archers get together to produce a wally or something a bit dopidiculous. Like that word.

Eskimo Nell ***Bell***
Even though telephones don't ring any more, people are still inclined to give each other an 'Eskimo'.

Feargal Sharkey ***Darkie***

Based on a white Irish singer in reference to a black person. Strange eh?

Finger & Thumb ***1 Drum***

Originally applied to a road, for which drum is a traveller's term, picked up by tramps who would 'hit the finger'. Can also apply to what accompanies the 'old Joanna' down the pub.

2 Mum

Used only in the third party, e.g., 'My old finger's getting on a bit but she's all there with her cough drops.'

3 Rum

An old but quite common piece amongst rum drinkers.

4 Chum

Uncommon use of a well-used term.

Fish & Shrimp ***Pimp***
An American piece that only made it over here on a small scale. In backslang, pimp becomes 'peemip'.

Fish & Tank ***Bank***
An underworld term for a likely target.

Five Acre Farm ***Arm***
An archaic piece that has long since been ploughed over. Coined when farm land wasn't as far from the centre of London as it is now.

Five Star Nap ***Jap***
A very old term based on the (old) *Star* newspaper's top racing tip.

Five to Two ***1 Jew***
A racecourse term, based on these odds, where Jews are an integral part of the scene whether as bookmakers or punters.

2 Shoe(s)
A worn-out piece that never came in for repair.

Fly My Kite *Light*
Ancient and lost to the wind. 'Got a fly me?' was a request for a match.

Fly Tipper *Nipper (Child)*
A piece to be used in the first element, i.e., 'How's the flies?' Which puts kids on the same plane of peskiness as the insect.

Forrest Gump *Dump*
A contemporary reference to defecation, to go for a 'Forrest' is to squeeze one out. Based on an Oscar-winning film, it can also refer to a dive.

Fortnum & Mason *Basin*
The Piccadilly store lends its name to a container and more mockingly to a short back and sides. Such a haircut is a 'Fortnum cut'.

Forty-Four *Whore*
An old reference to a prostitute, a successful one probably, if this is her chest size.

Frank Bough *Off*
Refers to food, especially milk, that is on the turn, whereby rank scoff becomes Frank Bough. Young people use it in relation to leaving, e.g., 'Time I was . . . .'

Frankie Fraser *Razor*
Fittingly based on the name of a well-known villain turned film and television personality, who was noted for his use of the barber's tool as a weapon.

Frank Zappa ***Crapper (Lavatory)***
The founder member of The Mothers of Invention rockband (1940-93) comes in as the seat of necessity.

Frazer Nash ***Slash (Urinate)***
Formed on the name of the car makers of the twenties and thirties, who in recent years were making electric rickshaws. The term has been running a long time, much like a modern Chinese cabbie will be if he ever gets stuck in gear.

Friar Tuck ***Luck***
Of secondary usage but could be used in conjunction with Fuck, i.e., 'Thank the monk for that bit of Friar Tuck.'

Fried Bread ***Dead***
Quite old but seldom used alternative to the very common Brown Bread.

Fried Egg(s) ***Leg(s)***
An always used in full example, a variation on several terms with eggs on the menu.

Frog Spawn ***Horn (Erection)***
'A frog on' for short, or not so short, as the case may be.

Gamble and Procter ***Doctor***
Loosely based on the pharmaceutical company Procter and Gamble which is loosely connected with healthcare.

Garden Gate ***1 Eight***
A bingo term and also £8 is a 'garden'.

2 Magistrate
Old but still used as in 'going up before the garden'.

3 Mate
A piece that started life in the Merchant Navy as a reference to the first officer.

Garden Hop ***Shop (Inform)***
A very old piece of thieves' jargon relating to betrayal that is suggestive of a Grasshopper.

Gary Ablett *Tablet*
Modern piece from the world of the young drug taker, which is based on a Birmingham City footballer who made his name kicking a pill around for Liverpool.

Gary Glitter *Shitter (Anus)*
Appears to be quite fitting seeing as how the self-proclaimed leader makes a living out of rock 'n' roll. (Rock 'n' roll - hole)

Gary Lineker *Vinegar*
People were actually sprinkling their chips with 'Gary' before the former England footballer's salt and Lineker crisps adverts appeared on TV.

Gay & Hearty *Party*
An old-fashioned term for the days when gay meant happy. The term would have aptly described a knees-up.

Geoff Hurst *First*
England's World Cup winning footballer becomes a first-class honours degree at university.

Germaine Greer *Beer*
One of a kotchel of terms that have emanated from the middle classes in recent years. Based on the Australian feminist, journalist, TV panellist and probably several other 'ists'.

Gianluca Vialli *Charlie (Cocaine)*
A very recent example based on Chelsea's Italian player-manager, a striker who has been getting up the noses of opposing defenders for years.

Gilbey's Gin *Chin*
A boxer's downfall may be a glass Gilbey's.

Ginger Beer ***Engineer***
A naval term.

Giorgio Armani ***Sarnie (Sandwich)***
A piece that is in vogue at the moment, after the Italian fashion designer who strives to be in vogue all the time.

Gipsy's Kiss ***Piss***
Very old and very common for a drinker to leave his beer to go for a 'gipsy's', the noble art of chasing the dog-end down the drain.

Give & Get ***Bet***
The origin of this speaks for itself. You give the bookie your money and if you're lucky you get your winnings. Although the most common scenario is you give him your money and he gets to keep it.

Gloria Gaynors ***Trainers***
Footwear based on an American singer whose records were aimed, aptly enough, directly at people's feet. If you are looking for any 'sole singer' jokes, make 'em up yourself.

Glory Be ***Tea***
An occasionally brewed alternative to Rosie Lee which has often been spouted in connection with an evening meal, e.g., 'Wash your hands your glory be's on the table.'

God Almighty ***Nightie***
Probably after one of those sexy, not-to-be-slept-in jobs that get men drooling and taking the Lord's name in vain. A repeatedly postponed event is said to be on and off like a bride's God Almighty.

God Damn ***Jam***
Has been spread on Holy Ghost since the Lord only knows.

Goldie Hawn ***Prawn***
A recent and much tastier update of Frankie Vaughan based on the American film actress.

Goldilocks ***Pox***
One of many references to VD, this one the type caught through sharing a bed with an infected bear or three.

Golliwog (gy) ***Fog(gy)***
When you can't see your hand in front of your face, you've either got your eyes closed or it's 'bloody golly'.

Gonzo the Great ***State***
Refers to a state of drunkenness, e.g., 'You was in a right Gonzo you last night.' Based on a *Muppet Show* regular.

Good & Bad ***Dad***
An old term for the old man.

Gooseberry Tart ***1 Fart***
Pip or poomp, rumble or stumble, trump or grunt. Whichever way you drop it, it's a 'gooseberry'.

2 Heart
One of the many terms making this rhyme for the pump.

Gospel Oak ***Joke***
Formed on the name of an area of NW London and about as common as a Gospel Oak on *EastEnders* these days.

Grapevine ***Line***
An old and probably unused example for a clothes line which may make a comeback as a rival to PATSY CLINE (qv).

Greville Starkey ***Darkie***
This ex-jockey was a forerunner to FEARGAL SHARKEY (qv).

Grimsby Docks ***Socks***
With all the docks in London to choose from this seems an unlikely piece. Unless it concerns footwear that reeks of dead fish.

Growl and Grunt ***Cunt***
Exactly the same usage as GASP & GRUNT (qv).

Guinea Pig ***Wig***
Most commonly heard rolling off the tongue of a piss taker at the sight of a ghastly gagga that resembles a small furry animal, e.g. ,'Cop the gink with the guinea pig on his head.'

Hackney Wick *Prick (Penis)*
Given Hackney's location in East London, it's a puzzle as to why this is of secondary usage to the widely known Hampton Wick, for what in backslang is the 'kaykirp'.

Haddock & Bloater *Motor*
Comes from a time before King Car ruled.

Half of Marge *Sarge*
An underworld reference to one who leaves a nasty taste in the mouth. A police sergeant.

Hammer & Discus *Whiskers*
Facial hair, probably as grown by East European athletes of yore who swept the board at chucking heavy objects great distances events. The men weren't bad either.

Handicap Chase ***Face***
Usually employed when attacking a custard-curdling gaseech, e.g.,'Look at the handicap on that poor sod.'

Hangnail ***Snail***
Not the mollusc but a slow, dawdling person, especially the pain behind the wheel of a car with dead flies on the *rear* window.

Hank Marvin ***Starving***
The name of this guitarist was possibly first uttered in an RS sense by a hungry dieter who was a shadow of his former self.

Hannibal Lecter ***(Ticket) Inspector***
The scourge of the fare dodger based on the character who is on a different train to everyone else as far as 'fare' is concerned.

Haricot Bean ***Queen***
A theatrical piece for an overt homosexual.

Harpoon ***Spoon***
An old term that was occasionally fired in the docks at mobile time.

Harris Tweed ***Weed***
A term for the skinny little ineffectual type, often the butt of a bully. He'd do well to remember that when the bullied stand up the bully stands down. Sometimes.

Harry Dash ***Flash***
Lairy people may acquire this nickname.

Harry Nash ***Cash***
An old docker's term, appropriately based on a

wages clerk in the industry.

Harry Ronce *Ponce*
Another 'ecnop' from the family Ronce.

Hearth Rug *1 Bug*
An ancient piece which may make a comeback, as the vermin has, in insanitary hotels.

2 Mug
Is equally old in reference to a fool.

Heavenly Bliss *Kiss*
Old, originally American example which is apt, especially when not confined to a mouth-to-mouth arrangement.

Henley Regatta *Natter*
An old source of friction between man and wife is when he's waiting for his dinner and she's having a 'Henley' with the woman next door.

Henrietta *Letter*
Girl who gets addressed as a boy when shortened to 'enry.

Henry Fonda *Honda*
Called after the American film star (1905–82) and limited to would-be taxi drivers doing the knowledge. It refers to the Honda 90 motorcycle, the most common knolly bike.

Herbie Hides *Strides*
A new, young 'erbert's name for a pair of gam cases based on the heavyweight boxer, holder of a version of the world title.

Hickory Dickory Dock *Clock*
Extended version of Dickory Dock, known as a 'hickory dickory'.

Hi Diddle Diddle *Fiddle*
A violin, as played by a hi diddle diddler.

Hit & Run *Sun*
Fittingly suggestive of the fleeting appearances put in by the sun during a typical British summer, like the one of 1998. Without the need for a sun hat this year I dug out my poet's hat from the bottom of the coal cupboard and came up with this:

The Sun - British Tour '98
Burning hot, it sets with the coming of night
Inferior beings depend on its might
Great fiery mass that circles the sky
Controls man's existence, he has no reply
Infinite power, yet strangely forbidden
In summertime to the people of Britain

Hod of Mortar *Porter*
Archaic expression that must have gone off by now, regarding a type of beer that is now only served at beer festivals.

Hokey Cokey *Karaoke*
A modern term for the pub entertainment much loved by the lager and 'I Will Survive' brigade. The more discerning will do the 'okey cokey, turn around and leave.

Holyfield's Ear *Year*
A very recent piece based on the 1997 world heavyweight title fight between Evander Holyfield and Mike Tyson, in which Tyson seemingly tried to ascertain whether or not a boxer's ear actually

tasted like cauliflower. For this act of cannibalism Iron Mike received a lifetime ban from boxing but was granted leave to re-apply for his licence 12 months later. A year, therefore, quickly became an 'olyfields.

Home on the Range — ***Strange***

Anything out of the ordinary or unusual may be described as 'very home on the range'. Like seeing George Best drinking from a cup, for example. Based on an old cowboy song.

Hong Kong — ***1 Pong***

Not sure if this is apt because I've never been there, but pong is Chinese for smell isn't it?

2 Wrong

When a plan goes boss-eyed it may be said 'It seemed like a good idea but it's all gone Hong Kong.'

Hopscotch — ***Watch***

With a leap in time the children's game continues the kiddie connection for what used to be known in the underworld as a toy. If connected to a chain it was a toy and tackle.

Horn of Plenty — ***Twenty***

One of a cornucopia of terms from an old bingo game.

Hors d'Oeuvres — ***Nerves***

Rarely served middle-class version of the Cockney West Ham Reserves.

House to Let — ***Bet***

Oldish but never really got moving. Unheard of now.

How's Your Father ***Palaver***
Anything complicated or bothersome is referred to as 'a right old how's your father'.

Hundred to Eight ***Plate***
It's a funny fact of life that you may have an old plate for years and all the time you've got it that's all it is, an 'old hundred to eight'. But as soon as it gets smashed it becomes an antique. Hundred to eight is bookmakers' odds for 12½/1.

Hurricane Lamp ***Tramp***
The second element gets blown away here, leaving vagrants, methers, dossers, gentlemen of the road etc. as 'hurricanes'.

Hydraulics ***Bollocks***
'What a load of hydraulics.' A colourful way of expressing disbelief. The dictionary defines hydraulics as 'the science of the conveyance of liquids through pipes etc, especially as a motive power.' Apt then that a carefully aimed boot would have a serious effect on this.

I Desire — ***Fire***
Pre-central heating piece for the traditional house warmer that was known as an 'I de'.

Ilie Nastase — ***Carzey (Lavatory)***
Based on the Romanian tennis player whose on-court antics and outbursts seemed designed to take the piss out of his opponents and scare the shit out of umpires.

In & Out

1 Snout
Applies to both the nose and to a cigarette.

2 Stout
Refers not to size but that which comes in a bottle.

3 Tout
Originally referred to a person who made a living selling tips to racecourse punters. Now, also, applies to a seller of exorbitantly priced tickets at any venue.

4 Spout
Applies to something ruined or rendered useless and so is always prefixed 'up the'. Also a pregnant woman is 'Up the in & out'.

Indian Charm(s) ***Arm(s)***
An Oriental rival to LUCKY CHARM (qv) that would seem to go nicely hand in foot with MYSTIC MEG (qv).

Inside Right ***Tight***
An old-fashioned position on the football field relates to one whose hands are too big for his pockets, of whom it may be asked 'Is he playing inside right again today?'

Iron Girder ***Murder***
Not necessarily the top job, but more relative to a liberty taker or a spoilt child who is allowed to get away with 'iron girder'. Also used in the sense of outrage, i.e., 'There'll be iron girders if the gaffer tumbles what you're up to.'

Iron Mike ***Bike***
Boxer Mike Tyson inspires a term that wouldn't have been out of place years ago when bikes were heavyweight beasts of iron.

(All) Isle of Wight

All Right

Anything kushti manti is 'all Isle o' Wight'.

Isle of Wight

1 Right

Applies in terms of direction and correctness.

2 Tight

Refers to those people who are not easily parted from their money, and to drunkenness.

3 Light

What may be switched off before going to bed and asked for when you can't light a cigarette.

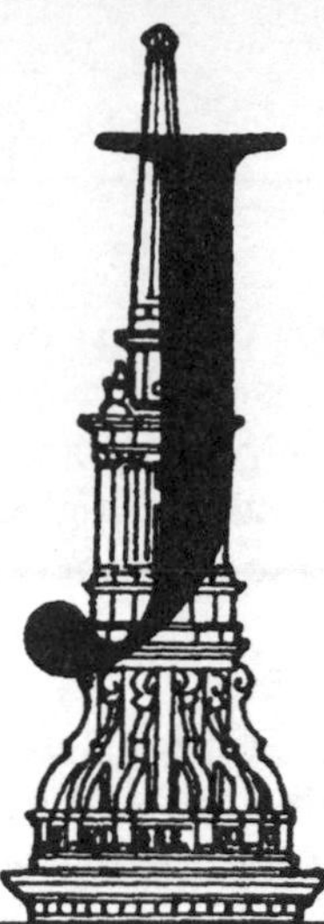

Jack & Joan *Alone*

More correctly on one's own. Either a misheard version of Jack Jones or could the famous Mr Jones be a century-old corruption of this? It's certainly a better rhyme and it would solve the mystery of who Jack Jones was. Nobody! Either way it makes no difference, if you are keeping yourself company you're still on your 'Jack'.

Jack Dee *Pee/Wee*

Currently treading the boards, how long it continues to do so depends on how long Jack Dee does. Since he is one of today's better comedians I foresee him being a star of stage, screen and urinal for years to come.

Jack Doyle *Boil*

A painful alternative in the skin eruption stakes to the more common Conan Doyle. Based on a colourful Irish boxer of the thirties whose gimmick was to sing in the ring. Had he danced as well, would it have been the lancer?

Jack Ketch ***Stretch***

A term in prison, courtesy of the man who curtailed many a stay by stretching the miscreant's neck or by putting an axe through it. Jack Ketch (d. 1686) was an English executioner whose name later became identified with the job of hangman.

Jackie Dash ***Slash (Urinate)***

Formed in London's docks on the name of a union official who found fame as a writer and artist. A council building in the newly rebuilt docklands bears his name, at the back of which drunks stop late at night for a 'Jackie'.

Jack Surpass ***Glass***

An archaic term for a glass of liquor based on . . . I don't know what it's based on.

Jagger's Lip(s) ***Chip(s)***

The singing Stone's salient features often provide late-night sustenance after a couple or ten pints of MICK JAGGER (qv). Of a dolt it may be said 'If brains were made of dripping you wouldn't have enough to fry a Jagger's.'

Jammy Dodger ***Roger (Sexual Intercourse)***
A modern piece based on a popular biscuit, which is apt if you think about dunking it. Known as giving or getting a good 'jammy dodgering'. The word 'Roger' has been used in this connection since the eighteenth century when the name was often given to a ram or a bull.

Janet Street-Porter ***Quarter***
A modern variation of BOTTLE OF WATER, based on the TV presenter and journalist.

Jasper Carrot ***Parrot***
That which sits *in* a birdcage and talks humorously, as represented by the Brummie comedian who sits *on* a Birdcage and talks humorously (Birdcage – Stage).

Jean-Claude Van Damme ***Ham***
Too long a term to be called anything but 'Jean-Claude'. Based on the muscles from Brussels film star in relation to that which is sold on the cold meat counter. If it has anything to do with bad acting you can tell him. I'm not!

Jenny Riddle ***Piddle***
The unsung sister of the famous Jimmy.

Jimmy Hicks ***Fix***
A drugs-related piece.

Jimmy Nail ***Stale***
The Geordie actor and singer comes in as a rival to 'British Rail' but if we're talking sandwiches here, he'll never be as apt.

Jimmy Rollocks ***Bollocks***

Another of the Rollocks clan for what in backslang is known in the singular as a 'kaycollob' which may be dropped in error. As with Johnny and Tommy, any of the trio may be used to complete the complaint. 'He's about as funny as a boil on the . . . .'

Jimmy Wilde ***Mild (Ale)***

Based on the former world flyweight boxing champion from Wales and formed when the beer and the man were in their heydays. Known as 'the ghost with a hammer in his hand' the diminutive Wilde (1892–1969) is rated as one of Britain's greatest ever fighters.

Joan of Arc ***1 Lark***

Not really used in relation to playing about but said after a narrow escape or if in a difficult situation, e.g., 'Sod this for a Joan of Arc'. Had the maid of Orleans been the maid of West Ham she would no doubt have said it herself when they lit the fire.

2 Park

Even in the best kept Joan of Arc there's a piece of dog's shit. A Cockney cynicism.

3 Shark

Another piece based on the fiery French heroine (1412–31), this one for the predatory fish, possibly a cooked one, comes from down under.

Jockey's Whip ***1 Kip***

To snatch a little bit of jockeys is to have forty snoozewinks.

2 Chip(s)

May accompany a steak or represent a stake.

Joe Baksi ***Taxi***
A defunct piece based on an American heavyweight boxer of the forties who found fame by coming to England to beat the then British champion Bruce Woodcock.

Joe Blakes ***Shakes***
A reference to the DTs, or the trembles of the well mangled.

Joe Daki ***Paki***
A recent example which has become common in the East End, but then so has the immigrant. In normal slang an Asian is known among other things as a 'sorefoot'.

Joe Erk ***Berk***
A twice-removed example, Berkshire Hunt, (Cunt), that has to be used in full to distinguish it from Joe Hunt, which is the same but different.

Joe Rook ***1 Crook***
A variant or mis-said version of Joe Hook.

2 Book
Specifically that made by an on-course bookmaker, this has been in existence since the days before a bookie needed a licence to set up his joint on knockers' row.

Joe Rookie ***Bookie***
Time was, anyone could set up as a bookmaker at a racecourse or dog track, so many would operate outside the bounds of legitimacy. Which would explain the association with JOE ROOK.

Joe Strummer ***Bummer***
A modern example regarding a sickener or choker, based on a rock musician.

John Cleese *Cheese*
Another piece of middle-class RS based on the comedy actor and writer. Refers to any kind of cheese, be it Cheddar, Stilton or Norwegian Blue. Or is that a parrot?

John Hop *Cop (Policeman)*
They say that you're approaching old age when the 'Jonnops' begin to look youthful. When judges start looking younger, you're there! Sometimes a John Hopper.

John Prescott *Waistcoat*
The deputy prime minister becomes the latest member of the Prescott boys to represent the third part of a suit. As in Charlie, Colonel and Jim Prescott.

John Selwyn Gummer *Bummer*
'What a John Selwyn!' As this Tory MP's daughter might have said when she was famously forced by her father, then agricultural minister, to eat a hamburger in public to prove the safety of British beef. A bummer is an unpleasant or disappointing occurrence, a bringdown.

John Wayne *Train*
Seems to have run out of track since the film star (1907–79) stopped shooting Indians from one. A post-war term, when you either got a BOW & ARROW (qv) or 'John Wayne' to your holiday destination.

Johnny Giles *Piles*
A more recent version of 'Farmer Giles' which is itself now dated. Based on the former Leeds and Ireland footballer.

Jonathan Ross ***Toss***
An updated version of the earlier Stirling Moss. For 'Couldn't give a Stirling' read 'couldn't give a Jonathan'. Based on the well-known famous person of no fixed talent.

Joynson-Hicks ***Six***
Based on Sir William Joynson-Hicks, a Tory home secretary of the twenties.

Joy of My Life ***Wife***
Often said with tongue firmly in cheek.

Judge Dredd ***Head***
A newspaper strip cartoon inspired a film and this contemporary piece of RS.

Judi Dench ***Stench***
A fairly recent example based on the British actress whose recent awards success would confirm that this has nothing to do with her acting ability. Her dameship just happens to rhyme with a bad smell.

Julian Clary ***1 Fairy (Homosexual)***
Modern piece that practically wrote itself, based on the gay comedian.

2 Lairy (Flash)
As appropriate as 1, given that his stage attire is blindingly loud. (Does that make sense?)

Jungle Jim(ming) ***Swim(ming)***
A term that lived and died in the fifties when a TV series called Jungle Jim came and went. Its star was Johnny Weissmuller, a former screen Tarzan and an Olympic swimming champion to boot. So the piece was apt at the time.

Kate and Sydney *Steak & Kidney (Pudding)*
A piece from caff society of years gone by. I seem to remember it from school dinner days as 'snake & pygmy'.

Kate Moss *Toss*
A modern reworking of Joe Loss based on a fashion model. Hence the unfeeling 'couldn't give a Kate Moss' and a dispute may be resolved by the toss of a coin, i.e., 'I'll Kate Moss you for it.'

Katharine Dock(s) *Sock(s)*
Based on St Katharine's dock which closed in 1968, which is possibly the last time this term was used.

Kermit the Frog *1 Bog (Lavatory)*
Named after a character from the TV series the *Muppet Show*, this is obviously of fairly recent derivation. Nevertheless, there seems to be quite

a few people hopping to the 'Kermit' when the need arises.

2 Snog (Kiss)
A passionate 'Kermit' will often give rise to a FROG SPAWN (qv) which may result in sprogs born.

Kettle & Hob

Fob
Whoever it was who first referred to a watch as a 'kettle' could not have dreamed of the arguments he was to trigger 100 years later as to the origin of the term. Some believe it to be this piece of RS but I offer it with absolutely no confidence. A fob is a chain (in full a fob chain) attached to a watch. It is also a pocket in a waistcoat where a watch sits. So why refer to a timepiece by its accessory?

Another theorist states that a watched kettle never boils but that's a watched pot isn't it? A slang expert informs us that early watches were cumbersome and resembled teapots. So why a 'kettle' and not a 'teapot'?

If an answer is necessary then maybe the best one is that, to satisfy a mass market, the cheapest and easiest metal to make the casing from was found in rag and bone yards in the shape of scrap kettles. Who knows for sure? Maybe Kettle was the name of some real life Victorian Del Trotter who knocked them out on the cheap.

Most probably a watch is called a 'kettle' for the same reason that a ring is called a 'groin', a brooch is called a 'prop' and a pound is called a 'nicker'. It just is! Just as it has also been called a 'turnip', a 'thimble', a 'toy' and a 'soup'.

Use this piece of RS if you want but don't bank on it being valid.

Keystone Kop

Chop
When the curtain came down on the crazy comedy crew of the silent screen, they endured in butcher's windows in lamb and pork form.

King Dick ***1 Brick***
An old example from the building site.

2 Thick (stupid)
'Ah, so there is a use for dandruff!' - A King Dickie, shaking one of those souvenir snowscene things.

Kingdom Come ***Bum***
In the days when corporal punishment raised cane in the classroom, teachers were known as 'flaybottomists', which means they would have flogged many a little 'kingdom' to Kingdom Come.

King Farouk ***Book***
Post-war term based on the former king of Egypt (1920-65).

Kit Kat ***Pratt***
A recent term for one who takes the biscuit, a twerp. Heard on a street corner as a long-legged beauty in a mini skirt passed two stalk-eyed young men:

First man: Phwoahh look at that. It shouldn't be allowed.
Second man: Shouldn't be allowed you kit kat? It should be compulsory.

Kuwaiti Tanker ***Wanker***
A piece that seemingly ran aground after the Gulf War.

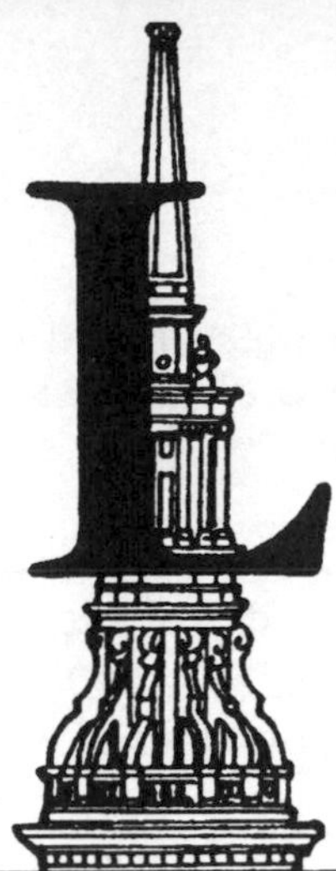

La Di Da — ***Star***
A theatrical term for a headline performer. Also used for the *Star* newspaper.

Lame Duck — ***Fuck (Sexual Intercourse)***
An old term for a plunge. One of the coarser, more chauvinistic references to a woman draws attention to her plungeworthiness. The more plungeworthy she appears to a man the higher she will register on his plungeometer.

Lancashire Lass(es) — ***Glass(es)***
A very old example but rarely, probably never, used by indigenous Londoners who do not make the rhyme. It refers to spectacles and drinking glasses.

Land of Hope — ***Soap***
An old piece that probably gurgled down the plughole years ago.

Lee Marvin ***Starving***
A modern piece based on an American film star (1924–87) who shares a rumbling belly with HANK MARVIN (qv).

Lee Van Cleef ***Beef***
A piece heard in a carvery in the shortened form of 'Lee Van'. Certainly seems to know his way around a dinner plate this old spaghetti Western star.

Leg of Pork ***Chalk***
A piece, heard in a pub, that seems to have hopped from the dartboard to the pool table.

Leicester Square ***Chair***
Always restricted to the first element, as in: 'Pull up a Leicester and take the weight off your feet.'

Lemon & Dash ***Wash***
An ancient piece that began life as a term of ablution before being taken over by the criminal classes. Pickpockets, 'at the lemon game', were lousy scrotes who made a living by dipping coats hung up in a public washroom. An alternative form of Lemon Squash. Thirteen and a baker's really.

Lemon Curd ***Turd***
The sweet in the street that gets under your feet.

Lemon Drop(s) ***Cop(s)***
'Watch it. Lemons!' A warning cry from a look-out.

Lemon Flavour ***Favour***
A friend indeed may do a friend in need a 'lemon'. Also a phrase of disbelief: 'You're gonna take up

exercising? Do me a lemon, you're too out of condition to get fit.'

Lemon Squeezy ***Easy***
The hard-pressed manager of a small boys' football team was heard to tell his losing side 'You're making it lemon squeezy for them, they're cutting through us like eyes a winking.'

Lemon Tea ***Pee/Wee***
A colourful description for going for a squirt, a pot-to-pan example known as a 'lemon'.

Light of Love ***Guv***
A convict's term for a prison governor.

Lilley & Skinner ***1 Dinner***
Named after the shoemaking company, this is a well-known term for the main repast of the day.

2 Beginner
Applies to someone new to a job, or a novice.

Lionel Bart ***Fart***
Local boy made good songwriter gets on the RS stage as arse music.

Live Eel ***Field***
An archaic piece that was coined before London became the urban sprawl it now is.

L. K. Clark ***Mark***
See ELKY CLARK.

Lloyd's List ***Pissed***
Ratstinking drunk as referred to in the city, after the trade paper of trade and shipping.

Lord and Master ***Plaster***

An example from a works' first aid box which doubles as a path in the labyrinth of terms that eventually lead to what in backslang is the 'esra'. *See* PLASTER OF PARIS. Extended to Lord & Mastered it becomes an expression for being boozed.

Loretta Young ***Tongue***

Based on the American film star of yesteryear who tongue-wrestled the leading men of her day. 'Hold your Loretta.' Keep quiet!

Loud & Clear ***Dear***

Anything overpriced is 'too loud'. That is how we should complain.

Lou Reed ***Speed***

A modern term for amphetamines based on the American singer-songwriter who walked on the wild side in 1973 and enjoyed a perfect day in 1997.

Lucky Charm(s) ***Arm(s)***

Based on those that are supposed to give evil the elbow and keep you from 'arm.

Lucky Dip(s) ***1 Chip(s)***

Probably formed because chips always taste best eaten from a bag.

2 Whip

Lucky the dip who picks the pocket of the one holding the 'lucky dip'.

Lumberjack ***Back***

Clever reworking of the word 'lumbar', especially when crying off a task because of 'iffy lumber'.

Mackerel & Sprat — ***Pratt***
As usual the 'sprat' gets swallowed up, as a pranny is a 'right mackerel'.

Madame Tussaud — ***Bald***
Aptly used when describing someone with less hair than a waxwork dummy. Also a piece of useless advice: 'Worrying about losing your hair will make you go Madame Tussaud.'

Maidstone Jailer — ***Tailor***
An ancient piece that fell off the peg years ago.

Major Loder — ***Soda***
An example from the racing fraternity based on a once famous racehorse owner. Refers especially to soda as a partner to whisky.

Malcolm Scott ***Hot***
A term from the theatre based on a long-forgotten female impersonator, known in his day as a dame comedian.

Man on the Moon ***Spoon***
A piece that must have begun causing a stir after Neil Armstrong's giant leap for mankind in 1969.

Maracas ***Knackers (Testicles)***
Fairly common piece most commonly employed as a mock threat: 'You'll get a kick up the maracas if you ain't careful.'

Marble Arch ***Starch***
A solid structure seems fitting for the basis of a multitude of stiffener jokes.

Margaret Rose ***Nose***
Familiarly known as a 'Margaret'.

Marmite ***Shite***
Probably a regional piece that some would consider apt. It seems you either love Marmite or hate it.

Marquess of Lorne ***Horn (Erection)***
A very old example that has probably reached its climax.

Mars Bar ***Scar***
A modern example of yob yab, usually used in relation to a stripe caused by a razor or knife.

Mary Blane ***1 Rain***
Drought conditions have set in on this one. It hasn't been 'honking down a Mary' for years.

2 Train
An archaic piece long derailed.

Mary Rose *Nose*
Most commonly associated with a super shonker, e.g., 'Cop the Mary Rose on ol' Hugh Jooter over there.' Seems to be from Henry VIII's flagship which was famously raised from the Solent in 1982 after 437 years on the seabed.

Me & You *1 Menu*
A piece long thought of as being RS but would appear to be more of a play on words.

2 Two
From a holiday bingo game.

Meg Ryan *Iron*
A piece of secondary slang for a homosexual (Iron Hoof, Poof). Based on the American film actress.

Melody Linger(s) *Finger(s)*
Has been hanging around for quite a while in the reduced form of 'Melodies'.

Melvyn Bragg *1 Shag (Coitus)*
Based on the name of the television celebrity and author. In 1992, a serial, written by Mr Bragg, was shown on British TV. The production contained many sex scenes and as a consequence the act of lovemaking immediately became known as a 'Melvyn'.

2 Slag
A modern version of Toe Rag in the sense of a contemptible person. Can't really see how it can apply to the game as a bagel girl who only goes with friends and strangers.

3 Fag
A recently rolled piece for a cigarette.

Meryl Streep ***Sleep***
The American actress comes in as a modern alternative to Bo Peep. The desire to get your bonce down is to need to get some 'Meryl'.

Michael Miles ***Piles***
Based on a popular TV quizmaster (1919-71) of the fifties and sixties, this is one of a daffy of terms for the dirtbox disorder. Which one to use? Take your pick!

Michael Schumacher ***Tobacco***
A recent middle-class term based on the German racing driver who has long been associated with Marlboro cigarettes in a business largely sponsored by tobacco companies.

Michael Winner ***Dinner***
Like many of these newer terms, this, after the British film director, was first served up in suburbia.

Mick Jagger ***Lager***
As used by stoned Scots. But then you would have to be a Jock to make the rhyme.

Micky Duff ***Rough (Unwell)***
Based on an English boxing trainer and promoter, this is generally used about the appearance of somebody after a heavy night's carousing, e.g., 'You all right? You look a bit Micky Duff.'

Midland Bank ***Wank***
A fairly common piece for DIY sex.

Milk Jug ***Mug***
An old piece relating to someone easily duped, one who stands the broads.

Milky Way ***Gay***
Based, presumably, upon the common perception of the effeminate male.

Millennium Dome ***Comb***
How rapidly these terms come into being. The construction is still in its early stages but suddenly a head rake is a 'millennium'.

Millwall Reserves ***Nerves***
In a caff, two men were discussing a miserable acquaintance. One was heard to say: 'He gets right on my Millwalls he does. Talk about happy to be depressed. I was depressed when I left him. He can't relax unless he's got something to worry about.'

Milton Keynes ***1 Beans***
Any beans can be 'Milton's' but this normally refers to the ones that sit comfortably on toast.

2 Queens (Homosexuals)
Mostly applies to establishments that cater to the gay community, a 'Milton's bar' for example.

Mini Moke ***Smoke***
Based on a small car, this modern term refers to *a* smoke, a cigarette which may or may not be a drug fag.

Miss Fitch ***Bitch***
An elderly reference to a spiteful woman.

Miss Piggy ***Ciggy***
Whereby the siren of the *Muppet Show* becomes smoky bacon.

Mockingbird ***Word***
An old piece from the theatre that has been killed by Dicky Bird.

Molly Maguired ***Tired***
Possibly Irish in origin, as the widow Maguire was the leader of a band of anti-landlord activists in 1840s Ireland. Her name was taken some 30 years later by a group of militant miners in Pennsylvania, about whom a film was made in 1970. It may be, then, that the term is based on the film title. Oh well, at least you've had a history lesson.

Mona Lisa ***1 Freezer***
Where else but in RS can a great work of art be mentioned in the same breath as a fish finger.

2 Pizza
One Italian dish for another.

Monkey's Cousin ***Dozen***
It's bingo time again folks!

Moonlight Flits ***Tits***
Women with extra large 'moonlights' are sometimes referred to as hunchfronts. At least they are by women of a more average size.

Mork & Mindy ***Windy***
From an American TV comedy comes this fairly recent term for a blow.

Mrs Doyle ***Boil***
A recent formation on the much blemished housekeeper in the TV sitcom Father Ted.

Mud in your Eye *Tie*
An old example that has been consigned to the wardrobe of oblivion.

Muffin the Mule *Fool*
A fairly old term for the sawney type who 'wears his best hat to paint the ceiling'. Based on an early TV puppet, this could also apply to television interviewers who thrust microphones under the noses of still sweating footballers and ask questions beginning 'How important was it . . . ?' Just once I'd like to see the interviewee reply, 'Well, how important do you *think* it was to score the winning goal in the Cup Final, you muffin?'

Mulligatawny *Horny*
A hot tasty dish would seem pretty appropriate for the hots, when he has a knob throb for her and she has a clitwobble for him.

Mums & Dads *Pads*
Those that protect the little legs of cricketers.

Mustard & Cress *Dress*
Always a 'mustard', perhaps in relation to a hot little number that perks up a Saveloy (Saveloy – Boy).

Mustard Pickle *Cripple*
An imperfect rhyme but a 'mustard' is a modern rival to the widely used RASPBERRY RIPPLE (qv).

Mustard Pot ***Hot***

The contrary nature of the English is never more apparent than when talking about the weather. It's too 'taters' in the winter and too 'mustard' in the summer. A complaint in the middle of sweaty, airless summer night: 'Ain't it bloody mustard. I could do the ironing with my feet.'

Mystic Meg(s) ***Leg(s)***

A piece that has been kicking around since the spaced out crystal-gazer first materialized on television's National Lottery Show.

Nanny Goat

1 Boat
An old piece that has sunk without trace due to the popularity of :

2 Throat
A common cause of a day off work is a sore 'nanny'.

3 Tote
Possibly the widest usage of the term is used in racing circles for the totalizator.

4 Coat
A very common term, frequently employed on a building site in the guise of a donkey jacket.

Nanny Goating

Courting
Not a great rhyme but a very old term for a very old-fashioned word.

Nap & Double

Trouble
An old piece that seems to have its roots in the turf.

Navasota ***Motor***
An old term for a car based on a ship that sailed between Argentina and London. A piece from the docks.

Near Enough ***Puff (Homosexual)***
An example from pre-politically correct times, when the close approach from behind of someone suspected of being a 'nine bob note' would draw the remark : 'That's near enough.'

Needle(s) and Pin(s) ***Twin(s)***
Like the well-dressed dwarf who sat on a tack, this is short, sharp and to the point. Pins and needles are identical, except around the eyes.

Nelson Mandela ***Stella (Artois)***
The South African president lends his name to a brand of lager, giving a whole new meaning to the phrase 'Free Nelson Mandela'.

Nervo & Knox ***1 Box***
Mainly applies to the 'goggle box', i.e., the television and is generally known as 'the Nervo'. Formed on the comedy pairing who were part of the Crazy Gang. Jimmy Nervo (1890–1975) and Teddy Knox (1896–1974).

2 Pox (VD)
Often truncated to the name of the first partner.

3 Socks
A piece from the theatre known as 'Nervo's'.

Nervous Wreck ***Cheque***
What many a pools winner has reportedly been while waiting for the man from Littlewood's to come and confirm his 24 points.

Newton & Ridley ***Tiddley (Drunk)***
A recently formed piece, comically based on the fictitious beer sold at the Rover's Return in Coronation Street.

Nickel & Dime ***Time***
An American piece that has found its way over here, generally reduced to the first element: 'There's no nickel like the future.' A procrastinator's motto.

Nicky Butt(s) ***Nut(s)***
A contemporary example in current use among the young, for the bar snack known as a bag of 'Nicky's'. Based on an England international footballer, this will no doubt see service as testicles.

Nigel Benn ***Pen***
Based on the former world super-middleweight boxing champion from Ilford, this is in the early rounds of its fight against the long-reigning Bill & Ben, which is well ahead on ball points and unlikely to be knocked out for a while.

Niki Lauda ***Powder***
The name of the former champion formula one racing driver was never one to be sniffed at in his heyday. Sadly though, it is now, as he does the rounds on the drugs circuit.

Noah's Ark ***1 Dark***
Cricketers have to up stumps when it gets too 'Noah's ark'.

2 Nark (Informer)
An old term which Spoonerizes very cleverly. Oah's (whore's) nark represents extreme despicability.

3 Lark
An old example that is used these days about as often as your right foot touches the clutch pedal.

4 Park
Not unheard of these days, people still walk their dogs over the Noah's Ark, and have been doing so for donkeys' years.

Nook & Cranny ***Fanny***
The dictionary gives 'nook' as a secluded place and 'cranny' as a crack. As a term for a woman's furpiece, then, this would seem particularly fitting.

Heard in a pub: 'You can't roll that tobacco, it's as dry as a nun's nook & cranny.'

Normandy Beach ***Speech***
The D-Day destination most commonly sees action at wedding receptions, when the best man goes over the top with a 'Normandy' designed to embarrass the bridegroom.

Nuremburg Trials ***Piles***
Bottom nasties known as Nuremburgs, where top Nazis known as war criminals faced their accusers.

Nursery Rhymes ***Times***
Refers to the top people's newspaper, which may cause 'Angry of Tunbridge Wells' to dash off a letter to the editor.

Nutcrackers ***Knackers (Testicles)***
An example to bring tears to the eyes of the hardest of men. Seems to be used as an extension of 'nuts'.

Oars & Rowlocks ***Bollocks***
For use when the smell of bullshit is in the air, e.g., 'That's a load of oars & rowlocks and you know it.' A perennial Jack of Tall Tales may be said to hang around Bow Locks. Also, to 'drop an oar in the water' is to make a mistake.

Oil Leak ***Sikh***
A recent piece for he who wears a napper-wrapper.

Old Fogey ***Bogie***
A reference to nose shit based on what was originally an invalid soldier. Lusting after a page three girl, a *Sun* reader was heard to remark: 'I'd eat her old fogeys I would.'

Old Kit Bag(s) ***Fag(s)***
Based on a First World War song, when catching a

smoking-related disease was deemed preferable to stopping a German bullet.

Oliver Cromwell ***Tumble (Understand)***
Comes from a time when the Cockney dialect would have produced a rhyme. Just as Bromley was pronounced Brumley and Romford - Rumford, so Cromwell would have been Crumwell, a suitable enough match for 'tumble'. Like the man (1599-1658) the term is long dead.

Oliver Twist ***Pissed***
Descriptive of folk who should not have asked for more.

Ollie Beak ***Sikh***
Just what the connection is between someone of this religion and the television glove puppet of the sixties, I don't know. But someone had a hand in it. In ordinary slang a Sikh is known as a 'raghead'.

On & Off ***Cough***
Obviously not based on the consumptive pest who always seems to sit behind me in the cinema and goes on and *on* coughing his offal up.

Ooh La La ***Bra***
A coy piece from a less permissive era, possibly from the stage.

Orange Squash ***Dosh (Money)***
Recent but seldom used except among the young, often linked with a lack of it. 'Got no orange' may be the result of a fruitless tap.

Orphan Annie ***Fanny***
Another term for a woman's fuzz-box, this time

based on a character in an old stage and film musical. A cautionary warning to steer clear of something less than kushti, a traffic jam for example or a pub where the guv'nor drinks lager, is 'avoid it like an infected orphan'.

Oxford Bag(s) ***Fag(s)***
You're getting old if you can remember when 20 Oxfords cost an Oxford. Based on wide baggy trousers, a former fashion (Oxford Scholar - Dollar, 25p).

Paddy & Mick *1 Thick (Stupid)*
Based on the names of the two typical Irishmen who have kept a host of comedians in business.

2 Pick (Axe)
As wielded by these archetypal partners in grime on a building site.

Paddy O'Rourke *Talk*
I have no idea who this is based on. Either it's a localized term after an actual person with the gift of the gab or it's the typical Irishman whose lip prints are all over the Blarney Stone, someone who could talk a nun out of her knickers.

Paddy Rammer *Hammer*
An old piece that has long resided in the tool box of discarded RS.

Pall Mall *Girl*
The word in East End dialect becomes 'gel', likewise this street in the West End has long been

'Pell Mell'. Said the right way, however, it rhymes with 'gal', which is more the show-bizzy version.

Pantomime Cow ***Row***
A light-hearted variation of Bull & Cow which refers to the type of ruck where nothing gets thrown but insults, much to the amusement of onlookers, who may later discuss it thusly:

'See that bull & cow this morning?'
'Bull & cow? More like a pantomime cow.'
'Oh no it wasn't.'

Paper Hat ***Pratt***
A typical 'paper hat' is someone who thinks a judo expert is an Israeli financier.

Paraffin Lamp ***Tramp***
Always reduced to the first element, often as an insult to those with truggy inclinations, ie., soap-dodgers and dirty-wacks.

Parker Bowles ***Rolls-(Royce)***
'Park the Parker, Parker.' As Lady Penelope might have said had International Rescue operated out of the Isle of Dogs instead of a Pacific island. An alternative version of CAMILLA PARKER BOWLES (qv).

Pat & Mick ***Prick (Penis)***
An elderly term for what in backslang is a 'kaykirp', sometimes 'kirp'. Hardly ever mouthed these days.

Patsy Cline ***Line***
Although based on the late C&W singer, this has nothing to do with dancing. The line in question is of white powder, cocaine. Patsy died in an air crash in 1963 aged 30.

Patty Hearst ***First***

Students RS for a first-class honours degree based on an American heiress and bankrobber. Kidnapped in 1974, she later joined her captors in the urban guerrilla game.

Pebble Mill ***Pill***

Based on a long-running TV programme, this modern piece refers to pills that are popped rather than taken as directed. A case of pebbles getting you stoned.

Penny-Come-Quick ***Trick***

Originally a fitting term for a con trick, which for a good artist was a quick earner. It later came to represent any kind of trick before disappearing.

Penny for the Guy ***Pie***

Seems a much more reasonable request than the more familiar Smack in the Eye.

Penny Locket ***Pocket***

The thirsty may be as dry as a snooker player's penny locket.

Pete Murray ***Curry***

The radio presenter is sometimes used as a stand-in for his namesake Ruby.

Peter O'Toole ***Stool***

Mainly applies to a bar stool which is appropriate enough given this Irish actor's bar-fly reputation. Incidentally, how come when famous actors get out of their skulls on drink and smash up bars and hotels they're called hellraisers, while the rest of us are down as drunken yobbos?

Peters & Lee ***Pee/Wee***
Lennie Peters and Di Lee were a hitmaking duo of the seventies and the term came and went with their hit records, a slash in the pan you might say. Some may still go for a Peters in deference to Lennie, a great East End singer.

Petrol Tank ***Wank***
Based on the vulgarly sung first line of the song 'Granada', 'I once had a wank in an old petrol tank in Granada.' Another reference to a 'hand shandy'.

Peyton Place ***Face***
A sixties term based on a long-running American soap of the time, which made famous faces of its stars. In backslang 'face' becomes 'eecaf', generally shortened to 'eek'.

Piccalilli ***Willie (Penis)***
A case of the pickle representing the schnickel.

Pickled Onion ***Bunion***
In normal circumstances pickled onions sit nicely on plates of meat (feet). Not at this table!

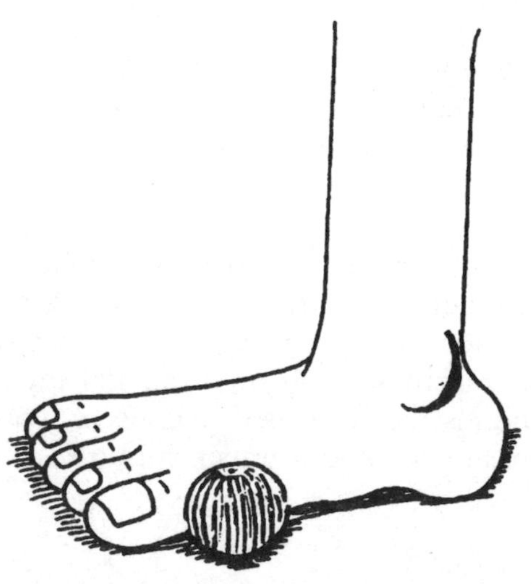

Pickled Pork

1 Chalk
One of many terms for the old but widely used scribbling stick.

2 Talk
An unheard example that seems to be based on drunken pigs. Well, it makes as much sense as pickled pork. What is pickled pork? Maybe it's a mis-heard version of Pickles & Pork, which sounds much more palatable.

Pie & Mash

1 Cash
In the cab and courier industry a 'pie and mash job' is a fare or job that is not on account.

2 Slash (Urinate)
Very common for those whose 'back teeth are floating' i.e., possessed of a painfully full bladder, to disappear behind whatever cover is available for a 'pie & mash'. Based on a traditional London dish.

3 Flash
A trappy, ostentatious, big-headed know-all may be described as being 'too pie & mash for my liking.'

Pig's Trotter

Squatter
A fairly recent piece for he who dips his snout in an unauthorized trough.

Plain & Jam

Tram
A term that is sitting on the back burner in case this form of transport makes a comeback.

Plaster of Paris

Aris
A three times removed piece that leads, via Aristotle (Bottle), to Bottle and Glass (Arse). Whereby a pain in the plaster becomes a pain in the arse, or an eye ache. 'Eye' has, for centuries, been a euphemism for the anus. 'Brown eye',

'blind eye', 'mind's eye' (that of someone who 'sits on his brains'), two eyes open and one eye shut (constipation), a sight for sore eyes (a lavatory in a dysentery ward), red-eye (that of one of the afflicted), are some that spring to mind. An ancient expression for that part of the anatomy, which treads the same path, is Roby Douglass, named after a gentleman who, apparently, had 'one eye and a stinking breath'.

Plate(s) & Dish(es) ***Wish(es)***
As written on greetings cards and signed by authors of books on rhyming slang, i.e., 'Best plates & dishes . . .'

Plate of Meat ***Street***
The original meaning, before becoming pluralised to dance to a new tune (Plates of Meat - Feet).

Plough the Deep ***Sleep***
An archaic piece that hit rocky ground years ago.

Polo Mint ***Skint***
The mint with the less fattening centre comes in as a protest of the potless, one who is 'polo' till payday.

Potato Peeler ***Sheila (Woman)***
An old piece from down under which may still have a currency among ex-pat Aussies in London, where women are more likely to be known as 'Janes', 'Jills' or 'Renes'.

Pot of Jelly ***Belly***
An old term of derision for a fat gut, which should be dished up in full, as a reference to a 'pot' speaks for itself.

Potash & Perlmutter ***Butter***
A play of this name was produced in London in 1914 and the term duly followed. You now have more chance of getting sunstroke down a pothole than ever hearing it again.

Pound of Butter ***Nutter***
Applies to any loon, from the wildly dangerous to the mildly strange, the eccentric who lives in a world of his own. And who can blame him? Given the only alternative.

Pound of Lead ***Head***
An old piece normally reduced to the first element, as in:

First man: (to daydreaming friend) Oi! Anything going on in your pound this morning?
Second man: Oh, sorry, my mind is somewhere else.
First man: Well, as long as *you* know where it is.

Press(es) & Scratch(es) ***Match(es)***
An uncommon example that was rare when it was common.

Princess Di ***Pie***
Current among the younger generation, this took a respectful dip after the death of the Princess of Wales (1961-97), but seems to have returned. Just goes to show, you can't keep a good woman down. You can't keep a bad 'Princess Di' down either.

Prune & Plum ***Bum***
From one of nature's laxatives comes yet another term for the breech, where the unwanted may be dispatched, i.e., 'Prod it up your prune.'

Psychopathic *Traffic*
A most appropriate example which has come into being in the exhaust-fumed wake of the motor car and the problems it engenders, causing normally rational people to turn into would-be killers at the first whiff of a traffic jam. A condition known as road rage has been used for several well-publicized murders.

Pudding Chef *Deaf*
An old piece that seems to have left the kitchen.

Pull Down the Shutter
An ancient term on which the shutters have been well and truly pulled down.

Put in the Boot *Shoot*
A First World War term that has had a sock stuffed well into it. It's no longer afoot, you might say.

Rabbit's Paw ***Jaw***
With Rabbit & Pork around, this seems rather an unnecessary term, old though it is.

Rajputana ***Banana***
Formed on the name of an old ship that used to commute between the Far East and London's Royal Docks. So maybe it was a docker who first declared: 'Making love in a French letter is like eating a Rajputana with the skin on.'

Raspberry Ripple ***Cripple***
A term that is often used as a mock insult to a friend who didn't act or think quickly enough. Based on a type of ice-cream.

Rattle & Clank ***Bank***
An onomatopoeic example from the days when the working classes dealt almost exclusively in coins.

Rattle & Hiss ***Piss***
A variation of Snake's Hiss, which is used in terms of draining the tank.

R. G. Knowles ***Holes***
An ancient term that lived and died in the theatre, based on a music-hall comedian who probably did the same, many times.

Rhubarb Pill ***Bill***
Heard in a restaurant:

> *Customer*: Got the rhubarb please?
> *Waiter*: There's no rhubarb on, sir.
> *Customer*: No rhubarb?
> *Waiter:* No sir, no rhubarb.
> *Customer* : Lovely, lovely!

Based on a type of purgative.

Rhythm & Blues ***Shoes***
Modern piece known as 'rhythms', after the music to get your feet tapping.

Riff Raff ***1 Taff***
A reference to a Welsh person which some may consider apt.

2 Caff
The great unwashed in relation to a greasy spoon.

Rin-Tin-Tins ***Pins (Legs)***
After the canine star of early Western films who was a bit lively on his 'rintys' but never seen to cock one.

Rip Rap ***Tap***
Generally known as 'on the rip rap', meaning on the scrounge. A twenties term for beggars and mumpers.

Roast Joint ***Pint***
Old Cockney dialect would have made this rhyme.

Roberta Flack ***Sack***
An American singer comes in to put people out of work.

Robert E. Lee(s) ***1 Knee(s)***
Generally the American Civil War soldier is disjointed to 'Robert' or 'Robert E' and often in connection with a painful one. Based on the commander of the Confederate armies in the US Civil War (1807–70)

2 Quay
An elderly piece coined by dock workers.

3 Pee/Wee
Another well-known Lee gets to strain the greens.

Robertson Hare ***Pear***
An old street-market term that has long gone to seed. Based on the English comedy actor (1891–1979).

Rob Roy ***Boy***
The eponymous hero of Sir Walter Scott's novel entered the RS catalogue at the end of the nineteenth century and promptly disappeared at the beginning of the twentieth.

Roger Hunt ***Cunt***
Sadly, it seems that anyone famous with this surname comes in for this treatment in RS. This former Liverpool and England footballer is no exception.

Roland Young ***Tongue***
Another term for the 'licker', based on an English

actor (1887–1953) who made his name in Hollywood and had it hijacked in London's East End.

Rolling Billow ***Pillow***
A piece that has ebbed and flowed for donkey's but is probably washed up now.

Romantic Ballad ***Salad***
Based perhaps on The Green Leaves of Summer or The Green Green Cress of Home, maybe.

Roseanne Barr ***Bra***
Thoroughly modern piece based on the larger-than-life American comedienne with the larger than average American underwear.

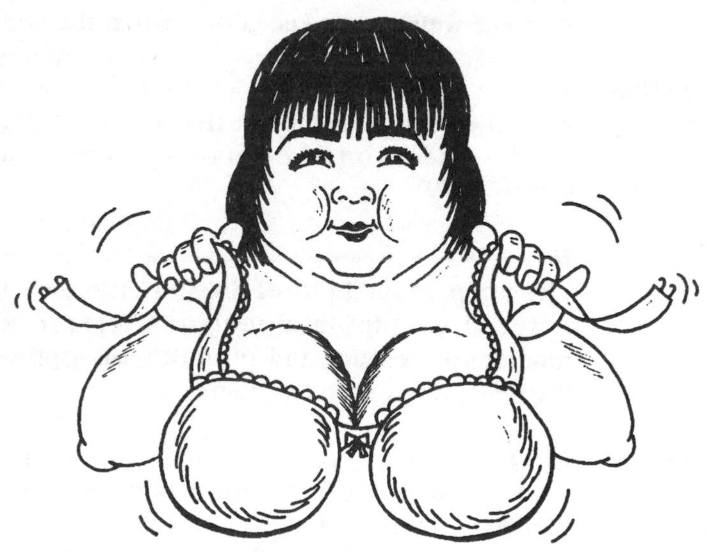

Rosie O'Grady ***Lady***
From a 1943 film and song title, this oldish term now seems only to apply to the ladies' toilet, the Rosie O'Grady's.

Rowton Houses ***Trousers***
Tapered to 'Rowtons' after Baron Rowton (1838–1903) and the lodging houses for ragged-arsed men that he funded.

Roy Castle ***Arse Hole***
The name of this all-round entertainer (1932–94) lives on as the 'reeking Roy Castle' of a persistent wind breaker. On a particularly bad day an offensively odorous orifice may be dubbed the 'one-eyed monster' which may draw the plaintive plea of 'Put an eye-patch on Cyclops will you?'

Ruby Red ***Head***
A First World War term, possibly a connection between red wine and hangovers. A case though of wine not getting the better of bread. Loaf of Bread is the guv'nor here, of which an interesting recent development has been 'Hovis' (brown loaf) for the noggin of a coloured person.

Rudolph Hess ***Mess***
Postwar term based on the high-ranking Nazi (1894–1987) and representative of failure. 'He's made a right Rudolph of that!' as Hitler may have bellowed, after his deputy's bid for Anglo-German peace ended with his being bunged in the Tower.

Russian-Turk ***Work***
An old piece that has long been unemployed.

Ruud Gullit ***Bullet***
A newly coined term for the sack which reflects this Dutch international footballer's headline-making dismissal from his post as Chelsea player-manager in 1998.

Ryan Giggs ***Digs***
Modern alternative to Ronnie Biggs, based on the Welsh international footballer who will never have to scour the streets in search of lodgings.

Sack of Rice	***Mice*** An old term from the docks, where ships carrying the term would have given passage to stowaway subjects.
Saddam Hussein	***Pain*** A fairly recent example based on the deposed Iraqi leader who has long been described as a pain in the arse of the world.
Sailors on the Sea	***Tea*** A long-winded piece that is only ever poured as 'sailors'.
Saint Clement	***Lemon*** An obvious connection with the old nursery rhyme, based on the patron saint of citrus fruit. Is it?
Saint Moritz	***Shits*** Something to do with the Cresta runs maybe.

Sally Gunnell ***Tunnel***
Mostly used in connection with the Blackwall Tunnel which is a daily source of traffic chaos and complaints that 'the traffic was backed up from the Sally to the Bow underpass'. Based on the world-beating athlete from Essex who, despite her retirement from the track, will continue to run under ground.

Sam Cory ***Story***
An old example from the docks based, apparently on an actual dock worker who probably had a name for telling whoppers.

Sammy Lee ***Pee/Wee***
Yet another of the clan Lee makes the water ejection connection. This time the former Liverpool and England footballer gets to splash his boots.

Samuel Pepys ***Creeps***
The English diarist (1633–1703) comes in to give a feeling of uneasiness. A place or a person may give you the 'Samuels'.

Satin & Lace ***Face***
No fearsome physog this, it would seem.

Scarborough Fair ***Hair***
A seventies piece formed on the title of a Simon & Garfunkel song of the period.
Two men heard discussing a barmaid:

First Man: I like her Scarborough, don't you?
Second Man: Yeah, but I wouldn't want it in my dinner.

Schindler's List ***Pissed***
A recent piece for insobriety following the award-winning film. Usually half cut at 'Schindler's.'

Scooby Doo ***Screw***
A piece of prisoner's slang for one of HM's turnkeys, based on a cartoon dog.

Scotland the Brave ***Shave***
Heard in a pub:

Barmaid: (to a male customer who has just had a haircut) Not much 'air about'.
Customer: No, you should Scotland more often.

Scuba Diver ***Fiver***
A 'scuba' is a current term for a 'bluey', time will tell if it sinks or swims in the crowded waters of RS.

Seek & Search ***Church***
About as suitable a term as you can get, where man seeks salvation in his search for the Lord.

September Morn ***Horn (Erection)***
If your birthday is in June, ask your father about this one.

Septic Tank ***Yank***
If an American is a 'septic', does that make an enemy of Uncle Sam an 'antiseptic'?

Sharon Stone ***Phone***
A new term that has been mentioned in relation to a mobile phone, e.g., 'Lost your Sharon? Well, leave me the number and if I find it I'll give you a ring.' Based on the American film actress.

Sharper's Tool ***Fool***
Given that a sharper is a cardsharp and that cards are his tools, this is a sublimely fitting term for one who will always find the lady when there's no money on it.

Shepherd's Bush ***Moosh (Face)***
An area of West London representing an area west of the left ear'ole.

Shepherd's Plaid ***Bad***
Must be from that terrible day up in the Scottish Highlands when a brothel caught fire and a panicking tartan-clad shepherd was heard to yell 'Let's get the flock out of here.'

Sherbet Dab ***Cab***
Wise to get a 'sherbet' after a sherbet.

Shiny & Bright ***Right/All Right***
Always be wary of a person who always makes you 'shiny'. If they agree with you about others, they'll agree with others about you.

Ship under Sail ***Tale***
A very old example for a line spun by a con merchant that is not likely to be heard these days.

Shiver & Shake ***Cake***
Usually sliced to a piece of shiver.

Shovels & Spades ***Aids***
Until they find a cure, the connection is sadly obvious.

Silver & Gold ***Old***
From the effect ageing has on the hair, as in the song 'Silver Threads Among The Gold'. In backslang, 'old' becomes 'delo', a word commonly heard in the fish market for rank goods. So beware the delofish.

Six & Eight ***Straight***
Refers to anything or anyone who is not bent or crooked, a piece mainly heard in the land of villainy.

Skein of Thread ***Bed***
A piece that has been totally stitched up by Uncle Ned.

Slide & Sluther ***Brother***
Sounds like the slippery one of the family.

Slippery Sid ***Yid***
A son of Isra-eel who gets his second bit cut off, as in the old saying 'You don't have to be a slippery to be a schmuck.'

Sloop of War ***Whore***
An old term for a woman of loose morals and even looser knickers.

Slosh & Mud ***Stud***
Originally referred to a collar stud but there's no reason why an ear stud shouldn't be known as a 'slosh'.

Sniffer & Snorter ***Reporter***
Conjures up scenes of old Fleet Street where the intrepid hack would sniff out a story over a snort of short. Or it may just be a case of someone who gets up people's noses.

Soapy Bubble ***Trouble***
Maybe from the story of the sex pest who got into hot water by approaching a plainclothes policewoman and inviting her to 'Hold it in your Palm Olive?' To which she replied 'Not on your Life Buoy. You're under arrest.'

Sodom & Gomorrah

Borrow

From the Biblical cities of sin comes the expression 'on the Sodom'. Fittingly so because 'Sod 'em' is a typical knocker's reply when asked when his creditors can expect repayment.

Somerset Maugham

Warm

The British writer (1874-1965) comes in from the suburbs in the shortened form of 'Somerset'.

Sorry & Sad

1 Bad

Very well-known piece. Anything in a bad way is said to be in a 'sorry state'.

2 Dad

It's a wise dustbin who knows his own sorry & sad. An example from the RS book of proverbs.

Spare Rib(s)

Fib(s)

Fills a hole when Pork Pies are on the whiter side.

Spotty Dog

Wog

Refers to any foreigner, black or white. Particularly, I presume, people from Dalmatia.

Sri Lanka

Wanker

After a newspaper headline which ran 'What a bunch of Sri Lankas', referring to that country's test match victory over the England cricket team.

Stage Fright

Light (Ale)

A theatrical piece hinting at the calming effect of a bevvy or two before a performance.

Stanley Knife

Wife

A modern piece based on the tool that seems to play its part in every trade.

Heard at the Ankle Club (a very low joint):

Man (to his upset girlfriend): Never mind what my Stanley Knife says. Do you think I'd have a slut for a mistress?

Stan & Ollie ***Brolly***
Famous more for their bowlers, this great pair of clowns would no doubt have placed their new umbrellas under their coats in a shower to stop them from getting wet.

Starsky & Hutch ***Crotch***
Based on a popular American cops & crooks TV programme, a deterrent is the threat of a kick up the 'Starsky'.

Star's Nap ***Tap***
Based on the bet of the day in the *Star* newspaper (the old one), meaning to borrow. It wouldn't have been uncommon to tap somebody for a nicker to back it.

Steam Packet ***Jacket***
Formed on a type of early steamboat, this has been sailing the seas of changing fashions since the mid-nineteenth century.

Steffi Graf ***1 Bath***
The German tennis queen comes on court as a modern term for a soak.

2 Laugh
The newspeak version of 'You must be joking' is 'You're having a Steffi'.

Stephenson's Rocket ***Pocket***
A wise businessman knows that you can't fill your own Stephensons without first lining someone

else's. Based on the train built by George Stephenson (1781–1848), which in 1829 zipped along at a breathtaking 29 mph.

Steve McQueens ***Jeans***
Based on the American film star (1930–80) of the sixties and seventies who had a fashionable image. He lived fast and died young but, unlike a pair of denims, he won't fade.

Stevie Wonder ***Thunder***
A new entry to the RS chart after the American singer-songwriter. A futile attempt may be said to be 'like farting against Stevie Wonder'.

Stick of Chalk ***Walk***
A variation on the chalk/walk theme that is lagging well behind the others.

Sticky Toffee ***Coffee***
A cup of sticky, as poured from the pen of a TV sitcom writer.

Stone Jug ***Mug***
Another reference to someone who stands the three-card trick.

String Vest ***Pest***
A garment that is worn in full at the approach of a nuisance: 'Look out here comes the string vest.' One type of pest to be avoided is the Wasp, who will tap you for a few quid and forget to pay you back. You have therefore been stung. Similarly a crab will 'nip' you.

Surgical Truss ***Bus***
Obviously made up by one who has suffered the bollockache of public transport.

Suzie Wong

1 Pong
Formed on the title of the 1960 film *The World of Suzie Wong*, which happens to be set in Hong Kong, a rival term to this.

2 Song
With the popularity of karaoke, more people than ever are willing to sing us a 'Suzie', making more people than ever willing to leave a pub before closing time.

Sweet Pea

Tea
A nice cup of 'sweet pea' is rarely brewed these days.

Swiss Army Knife

Wife
Said humorously at the approach of the other half: 'Look out, here comes the Swiss Army.' Based on the pocket knife with a multitude of attachments.

Sylvester Stallone

Alone
Based on the American film star, this is a contemporary version of some famous old terms. The modern youth is more likely to be on his 'Sylvester' than on his Tod (Sloane), Jack (Jones) or Darby (and Joan).

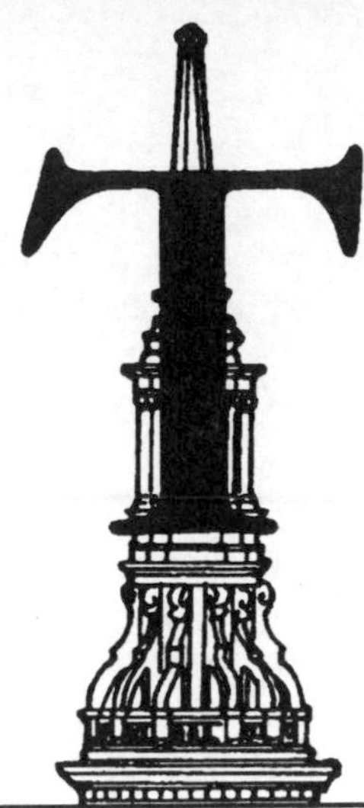

Take your Pick ***Thick***

An oldish piece, that may or may not have been taken from an early TV quiz show, concerning someone who couldn't pass a written spelling test. A typical example is the man entrusted with buying his works syndicate's lottery tickets. He forgot, and when, after the draw, it was announced that a rollover would ensue, he tried to placate his irate workmates by stating that it was just as well he'd forgotten as nobody had won it anyway. As one of his muckers was heard to remark: 'Is he take your pick or what?'

Tale of Two Cities ***Titties***

Dickens's classic gets the treatment as a 'Tale o' twos', and some time as a Spoonerism.

Taxi Rank ***Bank***

In the shortened form of 'taxi', this becomes quite fitting as the licensed cab is perceived by those aspiring to become a Brother of the Badge, i.e., knolly bikers, as a black money box.

Ted Frazer ***Razor***
Not quite sure if this is in the sense of a tool or a weapon, depends perhaps on whether there's a Mr Frazer or not and if he's a shaver or a shivver. My guess is that it doesn't draw blood by accident.

Tellytubby ***Hubby***
At last, a retaliatory piece for the long-suffering wife, who for years had had to put up with having numerous terms of RS slung at her, including, among other things, the Trouble & Strife, the Old Gooseberry Pudden, and the Plates and Dishes. Now her awful-wedded husband with his couch-slouch tellybelly gets his comeuppence. Based on characters from children's television whose names have probably been passed on to countless sofa-loafers. Still, better Tinky Winky than Old Ballsitch, as an uncle of mine was often referred to by my aunt whenever she had the ike with him. Then again, maybe not.

Terry Waite ***Late***
Based on the Briton who, in 1987, while in Beirut to negotiate the release of hostages of Islamic militants, was himself kidnapped. He was released in 1991, late by almost five years.

Thelma Ritter ***Shitter***
Based on the American film actress (1905–69), this has seen service mainly as a lavatory but has sometimes referred to the anus. Either way it's the 'Thelma'.

Thomas Cook ***Look***
As advertising campaign for this travel agency

suggested we should take a 'Thomas Cook' at their holiday brochure.

Threepenny Bit(s)

1 Tits

A term that survives even though this particular coin died of decimalitis.

2 Shit(s)

A double dose of the horrors, a piles sufferer with the Threep'nies.

Tin Hat

Pratt

As worn perhaps, by the pair of doughnuts who entered a tandem race under the team name of 'Schlemiels on Wheels'.

To & From

Pom

An Englishman according to Aussie servicemen of the Second World War. May now be said of our cricketers, who seem to go to the crease and from it PFQ against Australia these days.

Toasted Bread

Dead

A slice of black humour from the crematorium?

Toffee Wrapper ***Napper***
A reference to the head that should be reduced to toffee. I could be accused of nit picking for insisting that terms should be said in specific ways, but as Confucius would have said had he come from the Limehouse branch of Chinatown: 'Man who don't pick nits, ends up with itchy toffee.'

Tomato Purée ***Jury***
Whereby twelve good men and true collectively form, or one may be summoned to sit on, a tomato.

Tom Cruise ***Booze***
A modern piece based on the American film star who famously played a barman in the film *Cocktail*. Whether this has any bearing on his inclusion in RS is debatable, I'd say it's just because it rhymes.

Tom Finney ***Skinny***
The recent knighthood of the former Preston and England footballer rekindled a memory of a forgotten example that was a young man's put down of a girl who resembled a pencil: 'Nice face, a bit Tom Finney though.'

Tommy Guns ***Runs (Diarrhoea)***
Probably inspired by the effect on the faeces factory when faced with one.

Tommy Tucker ***1 Fucker***
An old term for a mischievous or spirited person. Normally said without malice.

2 Sucker
An underworld term for someone easily sucked in. One who is willingly sold the biggest dummies outside the Land of the Giants branch of Mothercare.

Tommy Trinder ***Window***
Based on the Cockney comedian (1909–89) who in his act used aggression tempered with charm. A master ad libber, he had a reputation for never being stuck for an answer. This would appear then, to be a perfectly fitting term, as he had all the attributes required to make a blinding double-glazing salesman.

Tom Tug ***1 Mug***
An old but rarely, if ever, used piece.

2 Bug
One of several old terms for the parasite.

Tony Benn ***Ten***
A term from the city of London where a Tony Benner is £10. Based on the long-standing Labour MP. In normal slang, £10 is known as a Pavarotti (Tenor).

Tony Blair ***Hair***
The present prime minister comes in on a wave from the suburbs; only time will tell if it's to become permanent. Personally I can't see it cutting down on Barnet's majority.

Tony Hatch(es) ***Match(es)***
A seventies term based on the composer of many TV themes who gained notoriety as a regular judge on the talent show New Faces, where he was invariably a hatchet man.

Top Hat ***1 Pratt***
Hard to believe that this word has become so acceptable, relating as it does to the vagina and to a fool in the same manner as cunt for which it is a variant. The term is never shortened and may be based on the annual upper-class 'pose in' at Royal Ascot.

2 Rat
Applies both to a rodent and a no-good cow-son.

Top Gun ***Ton (£100)***
A recent example from the City, based on a well-known film.

Top Joint ***Pint***
As with ROAST JOINT (qv) this would once have rhymed.

Total Wreck ***Cheque***
One of many terms for a kite.

Tower Hill ***Kill***
Aptly based on the place where executioners once wielded their choppers as royal heads did roll. The term doesn't necessarily represent the sinister. A worried passenger might tell a speeding slaughtomobile driver to: 'Slow down or we'll all be Tower Hilled.' A whimsical comment heard at a funeral... 'Well, if he hasn't gone to Heaven it'll Tower Hill him.'

Trafalgar Square ***Chair***
Only sits right when shortened to a Trafalgar.

Treacle Tart ***Fart***
A treacle wouldn't produce a sweet smell. 'In and out like a treacle in a colander' may describe a short visit.

Treasure Hunt ***Cunt***
The next time someone calls you a 'treasure', make sure they're smiling. Anatomically speaking, it's the booty of the sexual adventurer.

Trolleywags ***Bags (Trousers)***

An obsolete piece from the nineteenth century which may have some bearing on why the shortened version - trolleys - has come to represent underpants.

Trouble & Strife ***1 Wife***

By far the best known of all the terms for the woman who, in perfect circumstances, will be wooed, won and wed. On the other hand, she may be a case of bed, bun and brood.

2 Life

For many people this is about as apt as RS gets.

Trunk(s) & Tree(s) ***Knee(s)***

An example which would seem to have originated in Poplar where, incidentally, worked a Welsh teacher who insisted on calling the Cockney dialect 'Basic Poplavian'.

Turkish Bath ***Laugh***

Anyone having a 'Turkish' at your expense is on a wind-up or taking the wet stuff.

Turkish Delight ***Tight***

A 'Turkish git' is the stingy scrote who 'wouldn't give his shit to the crows'. A far cry from the generous soul who would 'lend you his arse and shit through his ribs'.

Two(s) & Three(s) ***Key(s)***

The number may well be up on this one.

Tyrannosaurus Rex

Sex

A bar-stool film critic was heard to comment: 'There was too much Tyrannosaurus in it for my liking.' And he wasn't talking about *Jurassic Park*.

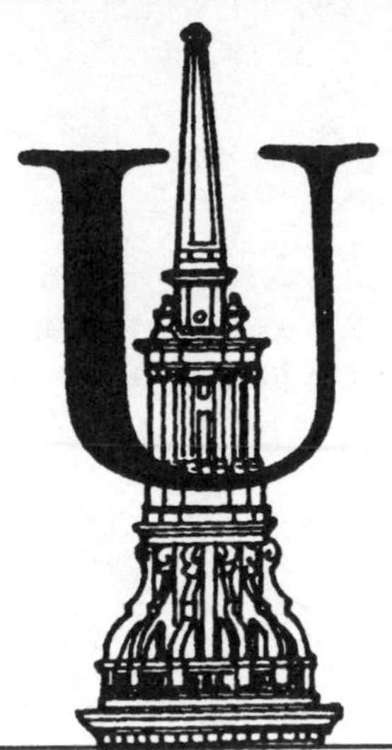

Uncle Ben — ***Ten***

Eyes down, look in. It's another from the bingo hall.

Uncle Dick — ***1 Sick***

Very common in relation to being physically sick or in general bad health. Often reduced to the second element as in 'dickie ticker'.

2 Prick (Penis)

Not to be confused with Uncle Bob (Knob). Same pipe, different tobacco really.

Umbrella ***Fellow***

Normally used in reference to a boyfriend or husband, e.g., 'How's your umbrella these days?' 'All right as long as he don't leak.'

Up a Tree ***Three***

Eyes up. Look out. There's another bingo caller about.

Up & Under ***Thunder***

During a middle-of-the-night thunderstorm, many nervous people are known to get up and go under the stairs.

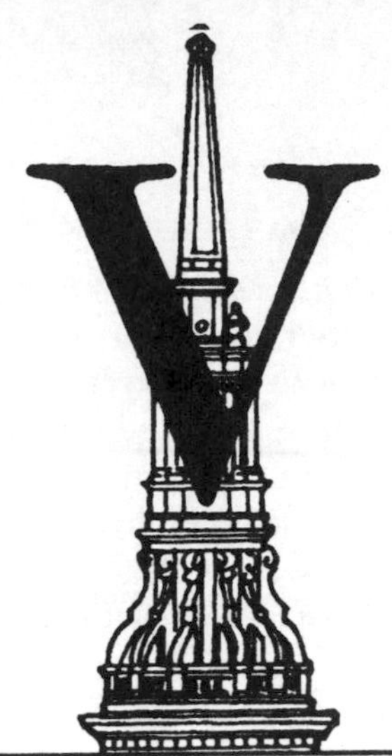

Valentine Dyalls ***Piles***

Known as 'valentines', this is based on the English actor (1908–85) famous as 'The Man in Black' on wartime radio. The term dates from around that time.

Vampire's Kiss ***Piss***

To 'take the vampires' is to get a laugh at someone's expense. Often this is light-hearted or jocular (after the well-known Scottish bloodsucker) but mainly it's to go for the jugular with a bit of spiteful fun poking.

Vera Lynn ***1 Gin***

Named after the songstress who won the hearts of the fighting men of the Second World War, this is by far the commonest of all the terms for this spirit.

2 Skin

A modern piece for a cigarette paper in which shit smokers roll their cacca bacca.

Vicar of Bray ***Tray***

Applies either to the tool of the waiter's trade or to the number three for which tray is the parlyaree version or to an old bingo caller's reference to the number three. Based on an ancient ballad about a popular vicar from Bray, Berkshire, who was infamous for changing his views to suit whoever was in power at the time. Sounds like a case of 'never trust a man that everybody likes'.

Victory V ***Pee/Wee***

As gestured by those who were on the verge of a bladder burst and just made it?

Virgin Bride ***Ride***

A rare piece based on an even rarer piece, although this was probably not the case when it was formed near the end of the Victorian era in connection with travel. Resurrected by servicemen during the Second World War, it was used ironically about a sexual ride. 'I had a virgin last night' usually meant that someone had paid to get their back wheels in.

Wallace & Gromit *Vomit*
The Oscar-winning duo who have made a big splash in the world of animation now make a splash on the pavement. The ancient term of disgust: 'You make me shit through my teeth' now becomes 'You make me Wallace!'

Wallace Beery *Query*
In the betting shop, a dispute of a settler's calculation is a 'Wallace'. After an American film star (1885–1949).

Walnut Whip ***Kip (sleep)***
To get a few hours' walnut is to rest your noddle for a while. Based on a chocolate goodie.

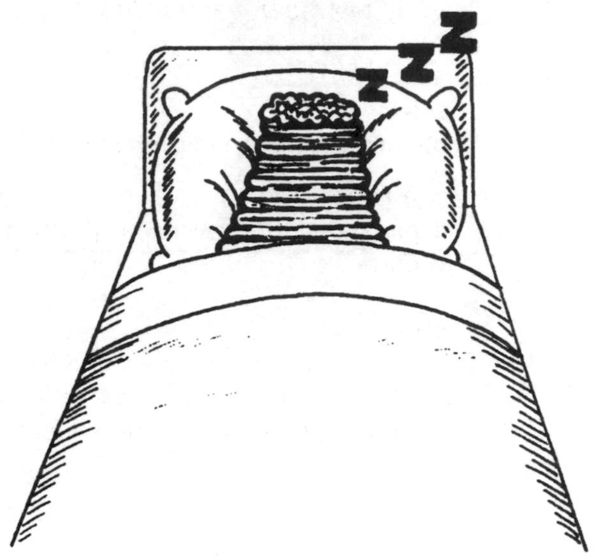

Waterbury Watch ***Scotch***
A old term that's been a long time obsolete.

Watercress ***Dress***
The garment and the donning of it, which means you get 'watered' after you wash.

Wellington Boot ***Root (Sexual Intercourse)***
A modern term for the sex act which is about as unromantic as it gets. Unless you're a rubber fetishist.

Westminster Abbey ***1 Cabbie***
May be derived from the complaint of an American tourist that, 'Whatever journey I made in

a London taxi I went past Westminster Abbey.' Actually it was a Japanese tourist but I can't type in Japanese.

2 Shabby
May apply to a rundown building or a scruffbag of a person.

Whiplash ***1 Rash***
Possibly one picked up in pursuit of S & M.

2 Slash (Urinate)
A rare piece but if you want to popularize it, feel free to crack away.

Whippit Quick ***Prick (Penis)***
Based on an old character from a radio comedy show, this is crudely connected with speedy sex, i.e., whippit in, whippit out and wipe it

White Cliffs of Dover ***Over***
Known as 'all White Cliffs' meaning the end. A symbolic piece really.

Wicked Witch ***Bitch***
An obvious piece for a malicious woman. Heard in a West End wine bar: Two men discussing the rise in fortune of a musician friend of theirs.

First man: I can remember when he used to cruise the streets looking for tarts. Now he's in America dating famous actresses.
Second Man: Yeah. A real bags to bitches story if ever I heard one.

Wilkinson Sword ***Bald***
A new term that seems to relate to the cultivated

spamhead look, i.e., the shaved head. Therefore quite a sharp example.

William Hague ***Vague***
A new term based on the present leader of the Conservative Party, which may be meat for the satirist's pie. Then again it may not. It's all a bit William Hague really.

William Joyce ***Voice***
An obsolete piece based on the most reviled voice of the Second World War, Lord Haw Haw (1906–46).

William Pitt(s) ***Shit(s)***
Not sure whether this is based on Pitt the Elder (1708–78) or his clever dick of a son, Little Pitt (1759–1806). But then who gives a William? As far as RS is concerned one English statesman is much the same as another, especially when they share the same name. This is a usually said in full, example: 'Don't take that out-of-date laxative, it'll give you the William Pitts.'

Willy Wonka ***Plonker***
A piece from a TV sitcom based on a Roald Dahl character. The original meaning of the word 'plonker' is the penis but in this case it's a fool. A willie's already a willie.

Winds do Whirl ***Girl***
An archaic piece that hasn't got a blow left in it, unlike the long-standing backslang version of 'girl', 'elrig', which continues to be heard.

Wooden Leg ***Egg***
Interesting to see the reaction of a waitress when she's asked for a couple of wooden legs on toast.

Wooden Peg(s) ***Leg(s)***
As old and outdated as a pegleg.

Wooden Spoon ***Moon***
Heard in prison as a reference to a month's stir.

Woolly Mitten ***Kitten***
Unused in relation to a little pussy cat, but to a lack of strength during an illness: as weak as a woolly mitten.

Woolly Vest ***Pest***
Apt in that a nuisance can be as irritating as an itchy undergarment. A pest comes in many guises, not necessarily human. It's a woolly vest when you have a sneezing attack on a Monday instead of achoosday.

Woolly Woofter ***Poofter (Homosexual)***
A juvenile piece that is common among the young but uncommon in that it can be shortened to either element. It is understood as a 'woolly' or a 'woofter'.

Woolwich Pier(s) ***Ear(s)***
An old term from the docks for nature's audio equipment, where the teeth of the wind get sharp enough to bite your Woolwiches off.

X Files — ***Piles***

Based on the cult TV series about a team of FBI agents who try to get to the bottom of paranormal activity and horrors of the supernatural. Unfortunately, for the whine-grape sufferer, the pain of the *anus horribilis* is only too real.

Yankee Doodles *Noodles*
Confuse a Chinese waiter, ask for crispy 'yankees' with GOLDIE HAWNS (qv).

You & Me *1 Tea*
An elderly piece that is still on the boil.

2 Flea
And this one is still scratching around.

3 Pee/Wee
'Let's you and me go for a you & me' Sounds like one for the ladies, who tend to water the plants in tandem.

4 Pea
Fresh, frozen, tinned or dried and blown through a shooter. They're all 'you & mes.'

You Know *Snow (Cocaine)*
The term 'snow' for cocaine has been around since the beginning of the twentieth century and this rhyming equivalent almost as long. Obviously RS at its most secretive.

Yours & Mine ***Nine***
Call a copper! It's another bingo term.